FIFTEEN SERVICES FOR SMALL CHURCHES

V. Elaine Strawn
and
Christine L. Nees

Foreword by Laurence Hull Stookey

 Abingdon Press

FIFTEEN SERVICES FOR SMALL CHURCHES

Copyright © 1992 by Abingdon Press

ISBN 0-687-12989-3

The Scripture quotation noted NRSV is from the New Revised Standard Version Bible, copyright © 1989, by the Division of Christian Education of the National Council of the Churches of Christ in the United States of America.

Other Scripture quotations are the authors' own versions.

MANUFACTURED IN THE UNITED STATES OF AMERICA

FOREWORD

Congregations with small attendance often suffer liturgical starvation. There is the unspoken—and wrong—assumption that *liturgy* implies large numbers of people and, often, a large financial outlay. The problem is compounded if the small congregation is located in a rural area or consists mostly of persons over the age of sixty. Then we add another set of what may be very inaccurate assumptions as to what is impossible, or at least impractical.

Thus the ample proclamation of the Gospel that can be communicated through the liturgy is lessened because we have been victimized by stereotypes. Much of that proclamation is carried within certain historic patterns, particularly those associated with the liturgical calendar. Small congregations deserved to discover the value of that calendar in ways often denied them.

What happens when parishes are cut off from the historic treasures of the church? Not infrequently, their members supply the innate human yearning for ritual by joining one secret society or another—the Grange, the lodge, or this or that benevolent order. Even when there is nothing inherently wrong with those organizations, the rituals they use may bear little relation to what Christians believe or to how the church remembers its past and presses on with hope.

Further, deprived of the liturgical calendar, such congregations often import something to take its place. In the United States, typically this is a civil calendar which then seeks to make church ritual out of Mother's Day, Memorial Day, Independence Day, Labor Day, and the like. This same civil calendar even distorts what is specifically Christian, so that Christmas is not considered to be the twelve days between December 25 and January 6, but the commercial season which begins increasingly early in the autumn and ends on the evening of December 24. And Easter seems to have more to do with spring fashions and flowers than with a divine act of cosmic transformation.

The solution to such difficulties is not, as sometimes supposed in the recent past, to come up with a totally new set of ways, promoted under the headings of innovation and experimentation, and presumed to have great appeal to a secular age. The better answer lies in learning how to use appropriately what has been handed to us by generations of Christians past, so that we sense our connection to and continuity with the great church catholic.

In truth, the real difficulty in such appropriation lies not in size or location or age of our congregations, but in a paucity of imagination or willingness to tailor generalized liturgical forms to fit particular sets of circumstances.

It is the strength of this book that its authors have imagined new possibilities through the adaptation of historic observances. By that very act, their work encourages (perhaps demands) further imaginative adaptation at the local level. The services presented here are not so much to be followed slavishly as to set free the imaginations of pastors and parishioners in each setting. You may well ask, as you ponder the suggestions in this book—"What else could we do to make time-tested liturgical practices fit into our own particular denominational and cultural situation?"

Liturgy is not the print on the page but the way in which the printed guides are enacted within the congregation. The failure to distinguish between the liturgical text (the words in the book) and the liturgy itself (the work of the people) is a grievous error which Strawn and Nees can help us to avoid.

In the process, we may be able to turn detrimental stereotypes upside down. In my experience, the newest denominational liturgies are being implemented far better in small rural parishes than in large urban ones. This attests to the flexibility of these parishes, though in large part the phenomenon is due not to size, as such, but to the recency of attendance at theological seminary by the clergy: New ordinands typically are sent to smaller parishes and are expected to "work their way up" to Old First Church—and by the time they get there, they may be very set in the ways acquired several decades before. Furthermore, when they reach these supposed "plums," the clergy often are between the ages of 45 and 60. Contrary to popular thinking, that—not the 60-plus category—is the time of greatest resistance to change.

Shortly after the Second Vatican Council, a Broadway play entitled *The Prodigal Daughter* was set in a Roman Catholic rectory; the subplot involved the interaction between its three residents: The middle-aged priest, the pastor of the parish; an assistant priest fresh from seminary; and an elderly priest beyond the age of retirement. The latter two were in league against the former when it came to implementing the liturgical changes mandated by Vatican II. The new priest was eager to put into action what he had just learned; the elderly prelate said, "Indeed so. I've put up with those stuffy old ideas long enough. Let's push forward!" The foot-dragging came from the middle.

That corroborates my own pastoral experience—and that of a pastor who recently reported that some years ago he had approached with dread a new assignment because the congregation consisted almost entirely of college students and persons over sixty. "Oil and water," he assumed. But he testified that, in retrospect, it was the most exciting and innovative parish to which he had ever been sent. We have overlooked the fact that if you live long enough, you get supple again, in a way the term "second childhood" gropes after but mercilessly distorts. May this be what Jesus had in mind when he asserted that we are to become "as little children"?

So make no assumptions about what you can or cannot do, based on size, location, or advancing age. With boldness and imagination, ask, "How can the riches of the tradition be mediated in settings which often have been robbed of the opportunity to appropriate them?" And let Strawn and Nees give you the first nudges toward answers suitable to your setting.

Laurence Hull Stookey
Hugh Latimer Elderdice Professor
of Preaching and Worship
Wesley Theological Seminary
Washington, D.C.

————Dedication————

For the Reverend Herman L. Strawn, "Georgie,"
whose great love and dedication
to the small church have
brought healing to worship
and made liturgy come alive

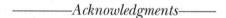

————Acknowledgments————

Thanks to Dr. Laurence Hull Stookey for the Foreword and for his suggestions; to Ms. Peggy Augustine and the staff of Abingdon Press for their work and encouragement; and to Ms. Sheila Voris Wild for her patience, her comments, and her undying support.

CONTENTS

INTRODUCTION

Words, articulately arranged and carefully manipulated, are the medium of our craft. As worship leaders, we feel called to insert ourselves into the center of a divine-human dialogue which carries hope for growth, change, redemption, rejuvenation, unity, and understanding. Ours is a business of constructing phrases and outlines in a way that best facilitates this process.

Our role, and the roles of the liturgical word and plan, grow in importance when resources are reduced to basics. Having served several small local congregations, we have run into "challenges" when searching for people to play all the parts. We try to create the proper worship mode when no choir exists to sing, when only a few people feel able to serve as liturgists, when there is little money for creating special sacred space; and the list goes on.

Somehow God seems closer when a Bach prelude sounds forth from the pipe organ or a hundred-voice choir is accompanied by a brass quintet. But these are images from our dreams. As pastors of small congregations, our *words* must provide a multifaceted mode. Our collects and affirmations, our rituals and benedictions must dance and sing. Our liturgies must proclaim themselves. This is not easy, especially when the person planning worship also is often solely responsible for pastoral care and administration. How do we find the time for additional planning while trying to accomplish the basics?

We know, despite our culture's emphasis, that a group's size is no reason to ignore or to underestimate it. But although statistics indicate that most denominations are comprised of small congregations, worship aids often target the larger church which has more resources. For this reason, we developed these services for our own churches and offer them here. They are for the small gathering, the small congregation, the informal study group, the first-time celebration of a special day.

We have chosen a very familiar, albeit unorthodox, format for this book. Early on, as we discussed the material to be presented here, we joked about using a "cookbook" style: listing the necessary ingredients and the proper procedure for mixing a palatable whole. After a time, however, our musing took a serious tone. We feared that such a presentation of worship would risk sacrilege, although this has been a useful means of presentation over the years. Only after much debate did we decide to proceed with what we feared. After all, is not the most sacred event of Christian worship a meal? Must we not all eat in order to survive? One of the beauties of Jesus' teachings and practice was his elevation of the common. He knew, and reminded those who forgot, that only things necessary to life become truly common. The most common thing, when offered to God, becomes very uncommon indeed.

And so we present this book in cookbook form, beginning with background information, then listing the necessary ingredients and tools for setting up the service. Each section concludes with an order of worship which places special focus on the theme of the day.

Four basic set-up formats are suggested. In each, a focal point is marked to indicate the central-theme object of the day (e.g., the baptismal font, the crèche, the eucharistic elements, etc.).

Sketch A is designed to be used for a formal service held in the sanctuary:

Sketch B is designed for a formal service held in a fellowship hall or social room. This also can be an alternative to Sketch A when the congregation is too small for a sanctuary.

We suggest that people sit in a circle whenever possible. This aids the feeling of participation and adds a sense of equality among the participants, in the eyes of one another and of God.

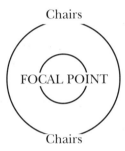

Sketch C is for an informal service held in a fellowship hall or social room:

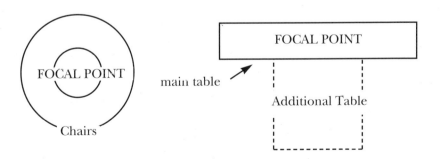

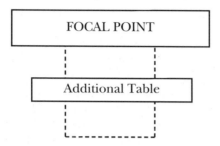

Sketch D is for a formal setting in an informal place, centered around a table.

We also suggest that, whenever possible, people sit around the same table. When more space is needed, another table can be added, perpendicular to the center of the original table and across from the leader. This formation represents the Greek *tau,* the most probable shape of the cross on which Christ was crucified.

The first Christian gathering was very small! *And* this did not seem to affect their worship adversely. With the firm belief that worship can be fun *and* meaningful, we offer the following suggestions. We've had fun working on them and have had uplifting experiences while using the services with our own congregations. Please amend them to suit your purposes.

Except where noted, the Scripture texts are taken from the Common Lectionary. The hymns listed were chosen for their significance to the theme of the day and for their familiarity. We offer them only as suggestions.

CHRISTMAS EVE

Apparently there was little general interest in celebrating the birth of Christ until the fourth century. The first liturgical celebration is dated around 335 C.E. Prior to that time, some groups such as the Gnostics believed that Christ had been baptized on January 6. Later, they cited Luke 3:23 as proof that he had been baptized exactly thirty years after his birth; therefore, they celebrated Jesus' birthday and baptism on that date.

Feeling the need to choose an "authentic" date for the Feast of the Nativity, the early church struggled. First, the third-century Plan of the Ages estimated that the universe had been created during the vernal equinox (March 25 by the Julian calendar), the time of the Jewish Passover. Thus Christ, the New Creation, would have been conceived on March 25 and born in December. Dating conception and crucifixion at the time of Passover had the additional significance of making Jesus' number of days perfect. Second, December 25 was the date of the winter solstice, by the Julian calendar. Thus the church placed the Advent of the True Light at the time of the customary celebration. But the North African church continued to use January 6. After much debate and compromise, the church settled on what we now know as the Twelve Days of Christmas, but because of differing calendar systems, January 6 still remains the date of the official Nativity celebration in some Orthodox traditions.

Advent (*adventus,* Latin for "coming") includes the four Sundays that precede Christmas. The church began this season of preparation for the Feast of the Nativity in the mid-sixth century. The first Sunday in Advent marks the beginning of the Christian calendar.

GATHER

- Advent wreath with 4 candles
- long matches
- crèche
- four liturgists/families (optional)
- paper drip protectors
- white Christmas candle
- enough small white candles for everyone
- choir/soloists (optional)

WORSHIP NOTES

Set up according to Sketch A. Place the Christ candle in the center of the Advent wreath, and move the wreath and the crèche as close to the center of the altar as possible. This is designed to be a candlelight service; it may be necessary to check local ordinances or with fire officials for any restrictions. If there is no ban on such services, instruct the worshipers to use extreme caution when lighting the candles; have them stand and remain standing until after the blessing. (This reduces any chance of getting too close to the people in the pew in front of them.) Advise them to use the drip protectors and hold the lit candle straight and still, while dipping the unlit candle to meet the flame. (This avoids the dripping of candle wax.)

If candlelight services are prohibited, either set up the service in the social room following Sketch B, or use Sketch A and have worshipers gather around the Advent wreath for the lighting of the Christ candle, the singing of the carol, and the blessing.

If it is practical and would not be too disruptive to the flow of the service, invite four individuals and/or families to read the Scriptures and light each Advent candle. These people should represent the diversity of the congregation as much as possible: age, race, sex, family status, and so on. They could be the same people who read the Scriptures and lit the candles during the weeks of Advent.

A short story which may be used as the meditation has been included in the Appendix. The Scriptures were chosen topically, rather than taken from the lectionary. Special music is optional and may be eliminated, or other hymns may be substituted.

ORDER OF WORSHIP
A CELEBRATION OF SONG AND LIGHT

PRELUDE

CALL TO WORSHIP

L: The Child in Bethlehem awaits us. Come and see! Come and see!

P: **As before, the electrifying expectancy of the hour bids us come.**

L: Leave your lists and leave your cards. Come to the stable.

P: **The glitter of the season fills our eyes, but we follow a humble way.**

L: Gloria in excelsis! The wonder of new life awaits us.

P: Emmanuel. God has come.

OPENING HYMN: "O Come, All Ye Faithful"

FORETELLING: Isaiah 9:2, 6-7

LIGHTING OF THE FIRST ADVENT CANDLE

CAROL: "O Little Town of Bethlehem"

THE VISITOR: Luke 1:26-38

SPECIAL MUSIC (*suggested: a Christmas medley*)

LIGHTING OF THE SECOND ADVENT CANDLE

CHRISTMAS EVE LITANY

L: Elizabeth expected to age gracefully, quietly, peacefully. She had long since given up hope of a child.

P: There is nothing God cannot do.

L: Mary expected to have a quiet, normal marriage. She didn't expect to be a key player in God's plan of Love.

P: There is nothing God cannot do.

L: The world is rushing headlong on a path of self-destruction. The peaceable kingdom seems as impossible as ever.

P: But even in our world, there is nothing God cannot do.

L: The angel Gabriel dared to name the impossible; Elizabeth dared to embrace the impossible; Mary dared to live the impossible. God calls us to fill the world with possibility. God needs us to help turn improbability into hopeful reality.

P: We are the Lord's servants. May we help it to happen as God has said.

JOURNEY AND BIRTH: Luke 2:1-7

CAROL: "Away in a Manger"

LIGHTING OF THE THIRD ADVENT CANDLE

SHEPHERDS AND ANGELS: Luke 2:8-14

CAROL: "Hark! The Herald Angels Sing"

LIGHTING OF THE FOURTH ADVENT CANDLE

A CHRISTMAS MEDITATION—"The Peaceable Kingdom" (*see Appendix*)

SPECIAL MUSIC (s*uggested: "O Day of Peace That Dimly Shines"*)

FOLLOWING THE STAR: Luke 2:15-20

LIGHTING OF THE CHRIST CANDLE

LIGHTING OF EVERYONE'S CANDLE FROM THE CHRIST CANDLE
(*Selected Scripture may be read: Gen. 1:3-4; Isa. 9:2; Ps. 119:105; Matt. 5:14; Luke 8:16; John 1:4, 8:12, 12:36, 46; Rom. 13:12; Eph. 5:8; I John 1:7*)

CAROL: "Silent Night"

CHRISTMAS BLESSING

L: The peace of Christ goes with us as we leave this place.

P: The light of Christ surrounds us as we go.

L: The love of God was born among us,

P: And has been rekindled in us here this night.

L: Go in peace, to share the love of God with all you meet.

P: We are sent in the name of Emmanuel! God is with us indeed!

ALL: Alleluia! Amen.

EXTINGUISHING OF THE CANDLES

CAROL: "Joy to the World"

POSTLUDE

EPIPHANY

piphaneia is a Greek word meaning "manifestation." Christians use it to denote the feast day that commemorates the manifestation of Jesus as the Incarnate God. Before the church settled upon the date of the feast day we now call Christmas, January 6 was thought to be the date on which Christ was presented in the Temple, and thus Christ's spiritual birthday. For this reason, the Twelfth Day of Christmas, or Epiphany, was one of the original feast days of the Christian church.

The festive mood of Christ's birth continues on this day when Christians turn their thoughts to the journey of the Magi. Those Babylonian or Persian priests, versed in astrology, presented their gifts to the Christ Child: gold to crown a king, frankincense to purify the air or a deity, myrrh to foreshadow the events to come. On this day, we stop to think of the gifts we can offer the Christ Child.

GATHER

- crèche
- 2 baskets
- Advent wreath
- wrapped presents or decorative tin boxes
- paper slips and pencils

WORSHIP NOTES

Set up for this service following Sketch A, held in the sanctuary or chapel, or in a more informal room with an altar. Enclose the slips of paper and pencils in the bulletins before they are distributed. In addition to the cross and candles on the altar, add the Advent wreath with all candles lit, and a small crèche. Gifts (either boxes wrapped in festive paper or decorative tin boxes) should be on the floor in front of the altar. Place the large baskets on either side of the altar or on the floor in front of the chancel.

ORDER OF WORSHIP

PRELUDE

GATHERING

PROCLAMATION OF THE WORD: Isaiah 60:1-6

RESPONSE TO THE SCRIPTURE

L: Once again, Christ has come to be among us.

P: Once again, we are blessed with God's gift.

L: Our tinsel and ribbons have been cleared away,

P: But the gifts of the Magi are still to arrive.

L: What will you bring to add to their gifts?

P: We bring our lives and our talents.

L: Come away from the world, whose celebration is over.

P: We come to the manger, where the joy has just begun!

HYMN: "As with Gladness, Those of Old"

PRAYER OF CONFESSION

   **O God of Shining Stars, you give us such spectacular gifts through-
out our lives. So often we take them for granted, and ask for more.
Forgive our greed and dissatisfaction. Shine in our lives as the star**

shone over Bethlehem. **Lead us to new awareness and appreciation. Fill us with the wisdom and determination of the Magi. Let us not be tricked by the wiles of Herod. Help us to see beyond our selfish desires to the magnificence of your glory. And, with the wandering astronomers, teach us to worship with our gifts, our time, and our lives. Amen.**

WORDS OF ASSURANCE

The Christ has come to live among us. God is with us now. Lift your heads and present yourselves as living gifts, knowing that the One who created you will receive you with love. Amen.

RESPONSIVE PSALTER READING: Psalm 72:1-14

ANTHEM OR SPECIAL MUSIC

PRAYERS OF THE PEOPLE with the Lord's Prayer
(*The Epistle may be read here: Ephesians 3:1-12*)

HYMN OF PREPARATION: "I Wonder As I Wander" or "We Three Kings"

GOSPEL: Matthew 2:1-12

SERMON

The emphasis should be first on the universality of Christ's message and mission, as proclaimed by Paul and by the visit of the Magi. Second, we should concentrate on the gifts we bring to the Christ Child. So often we denigrate our talents and think we have nothing to offer. Like the little drummer boy of musical fame, we think we must offer great material wealth, or operatic voices, or Mosaic prayers. Instead, all that Jesus desires is the gift of our ordinary talents. Can we gather the skills and talents we possess and follow the star of faith to offer ourselves to the Babe in the manger?

PRESENTATION OF TITHES AND GIFTS

Moments of Silent Meditation

Write the talents you have to offer on the pieces of paper in your bulletins.

Procession to the Altar

Please place your tithes in the basket on the left side of the altar, and your offerings of skill and talent in the basket on the right.

Affirmation of Faith

We believe God is with us, present at every moment. Through the life of Jesus Christ, God became human. Thus we learned how God expects us to live and to be. Because Christ was born in human form, we know that nothing, no matter how great or small, is beyond God's experience and understanding. Our God understands our frailties and strengths, our temptations and our glories.

We believe that Jesus sent the Spirit to be within us, guiding us and teaching us throughout our lives. We believe that our pledges of talent and love are dear to God and will be blessed with power. Amen.

Blessings of Gifts and Offerings

O God of the Nativity, be born in our hearts as we offer these gifts. They represent the best we have to give: our talents, our lives, and our love. We offer them for your use. Bless them and expand them, in the name and the mission of the Prince of Peace. Amen.

HYMN OF DEDICATION: "Go Tell It on the Mountain"

BENEDICTION in Unison

God has given us the most precious gift imaginable. We have offered our gifts in return. This exchange is done in love, rather than in duty, for God first loved us. Now we offer that love to the world in the name of Christ. Alleluia!

POSTLUDE

BAPTISM OF OUR LORD

The origin of baptism is uncertain, although we do know that it predates Christianity and the church. Like circumcision, baptism may have had its beginning in the Levitical washings. We cannot miss the importance of water in our faith history: The waters moved over the earth at creation; the flood waters cleansed the world of Noah's time; Amos talked of overflowing streams of righteousness; Jesus gave the woman at the well everlasting water.

Just prior to the Christian era, Gentile proselytes qualified for membership in the nation of Israel through baptism. John the Baptist used the ritual as a symbol of purification and preparation for the Messiah. He consecrated people in this way, that they might receive salvation. Later, he consecrated Jesus, that he might *bestow* salvation.

Peter viewed baptism as the rite which granted a believer admission into the church through reception of the Holy Spirit. Paul saw baptism as a cleansing by the Spirit, which led to a new relationship with Christ; it was the great rite of purification and rebirth into eternal life. During Paul's time, baptism became the sacrament which united the believer with Christ. For this reason, in most churches, it is received only once in a person's lifetime.

Until 604 C.E., baptism was understood as the rite of inclusion into the covenantal community. The specific significance and form of baptism were defined during the second century. Before 325 C.E., everyone was welcome at the service of prayers, Scripture readings, and preaching, but only baptized Christians were allowed to participate in the eucharistic section of worship. During the Middle Ages, baptism focused on the individual: The necessary rite was administered soon after birth in order to remove the stains of original sin from the child. Only with the modern liturgical movement is baptism once again viewed as a sacramental covenant that brings the believer into the community of God's grace. Once again, we are returning to baptism's important message of the equality of all believers before God.

From Hippolytus' complaints, we can guess that infants were being baptized by 150 C.E. That practice ceased during the time of Roman persecution of baptized Christians and resumed only after Constantine legalized Christianity. Immersion and pouring seem to have been the traditional forms of baptism (immersion has always been the form bestowed by the Eastern church). Through time, immersion faded from prominence in the Western church as parents began to resist it. Traditionally, fasting and an expression of belief were prerequisites for baptism. Afterward, the celebrant placed milk and honey on the tongues of the believers to symbolize the blessings of life lived in Christ.

GATHER

- baptismal font or bowl
- pitcher filled with warm water
- milk and honey
- portable container
- altar
- table

WORSHIP NOTES

Set up the sanctuary according to Sketch A; a small group might use the social hall or chapel and set up according to Sketch B. The central focus should be on the font, placed as close to the center as possible. (The altar can be placed in the circle if Sketch B is used.) In addition to the cross and candles, place the pitcher filled with warm water on the altar with the milk and honey. Beside the empty font, place a small table.

Immediately before the Litany of the Water begins, move the pitcher from the altar to this table. This links the symbolic water with Christ, while eliminating the need to get the pitcher from the altar every time it is used. Care should be taken to make the font as visible as possible.

During the litany, read the Scripture text, then hold the pitcher at a distance from the font and pour in the water so that the sound can be heard. Follow this procedure with each reading. Immediately following the pouring of the water in each case, the congregation might sing the chorus of a familiar baptism hymn: "The Rock Shall Wear Away" (by Meg Christian), "Seek Ye First the Kingdom of God," or "I Shall Not Be Moved."

The baptisms, of course, should be carried out as customary in your denomination. If children or adults are to be baptized, this would best be done immediately after the sermon.

During the ritual of Baptismal Renewal, carry the bowl of the font, or pour some of the water into a smaller container. Then walk among the worshipers, sprinkling the water on them and saying, "Remember your baptism and be thankful." The paste or pieces of milk and honey should be given to the worshipers during the final hymn. A recipe for the milk and honey can be found in the Appendix.

ORDER OF WORSHIP

GATHERING

PRELUDE

CALL TO WORSHIP

L: God has created a holy space and endowed it with life.

P: We are part of that life, called apart to be signs of the Creator's continued care.

L: People of faith, you accept a great mission when you enter these doors.

P: We are a covenant people, followers of the Christ and of the Way of the kingdom.

L: Come, celebrate the baptism of Jesus in the Jordan.

P: We come, as participants in that heritage.

HYMN OF PRAISE: "Come, Thou Fount of Every Blessing"

LITANY OF THE WATER

At the baptismal font, read from Scripture while slowly pouring water into the font: Primordial Waters/Creation—Gen. 1:1, 2, 6-10; Flood Covenant—Gen. 9:11-17; Amos' Streams of Righteousness—Amos 5:21-24; Jesus' Declaration—John 3:1-8; Woman at the Well—John 4:7-14. Following each reading, a chorus from an appropriate hymn may be sung.

PRAYERS OF THE PEOPLE

Moments of silence, prayers of intercession, and the Lord's Prayer

OLD TESTAMENT: Isaiah 42:1-9; Genesis 1:1-5; Isaiah 61:1-4

EPISTLE: Acts 10:34-43; Acts 19:1-7; Acts 8:14-17

PRESENTATION OF TITHES AND OFFERINGS with Doxology

HYMN OF PREPARATION: "Jesus! The Name Held High Over All"

GOSPEL: Matthew 3:13-17; Mark 1:4-11; Luke 3:15-17, 21-22

SERMON

Comments can be made about the symbolism of water: such a simple and basic element, yet so necessary for life. Water is needed both for quenching thirst and for cleansing. Jesus always chose the simple, basic elements of life—water, bread, and wine—for the most sacred rituals.

BAPTISM OF CANDIDATES

CELEBRATION OF THE RENEWAL OF BAPTISMAL VOWS

AFFIRMATION OF FAITH

I believe in God, the Source of all. I believe in God's continued relationship with the Creation. This Creator based creation on simple elements—water, bread, and the fruit of the vine. God seeks to meet the needs of this creation.

The relationship between God and creation was made more intimate through the life of Jesus Christ, wholly God and wholly human. In his teaching, healing, living, dying, and conquering of death, this Jesus guided humanity to the Truth.

I believe in the Holy Spirit, who remains an ever-present source of wisdom, strength, and love.

I believe in the church as the body of believers, dedicated to making the creation grow closer to the Way of God. We celebrate this church's life and our commitment through the rites of baptism and Communion.

I believe in myself as one created in God's image, who is called to serve and care for the creation around me. Amen.

PLEDGES TO GOD AND TO ONE ANOTHER

L: We are a people of the covenant. Abraham and Sarah, Moses and Miriam, Esther, David, and many others entered into a covenant with God, promising their lives to God's mission. Generations of Christians since have entered into similar promises, some even giving up their very lives. Why, O people of faith, have you come?

P: **We have given our lives to God's care and leading. We have lived lives attuned to God's calling. We stand in need of the Creator's nurture and leading. We recognize the need for a community of faith to share the burdens and the joys. We come to commit ourselves anew to God, and to one another.**

WATERS OF BAPTISM
The pastor sprinkles the congregation.

L: In our original baptism, we were brought into intimate relation with God, our Creator. In baptism, we make a mutual promise with God. Just as we are open to leading, so we require God's care. Let us pray:

P: **O God, in your unconditional love, you have been with us from the beginning and will continue with us until the end. Bless us with your Spirit. Be, once again, in these simple waters as we renew our vows, so that we may feel your presence among us. Amen.**

L: Remember your baptism and be thankful . . . .

HYMN OF DEDICATION: "Marching to Zion"
Distribution of milk and honey.

BENEDICTION

L: We have been touched by the Waters of Life.

P: **Common water has been transformed into Divine Blessing. We are renewed and refreshed.**

ALL: Amen.

POSTLUDE

TRANSFIGURATION SUNDAY

Six to eight days after Jesus first told the disciples about his upcoming sacrifice, he took Peter, James, and John with him up snowy Mount Hermon, close to Caesarea Philippi. The events which followed firmly established Jesus as God's "beloved Son," in the same line with Moses (and the Law) and Elijah (and the prophets). The three disciples witnessed Jesus as the culmination of God's revelation.

Transfigure is the translation of a Greek term meaning "magical Metamorphosis," which refers to a glorifying change in spirit and form. The cloud indicates the Divine Presence. The Transfiguration of Jesus with Moses and Elijah was exalting enough to confirm his Messiahship in the eyes of the witnesses, even later as they watched him suffer. This vision was important to the early church. As the early Christians struggled, the story of the Transfiguration gave them the same confidence it had given to Peter, James, and John.

GATHER

- walking stick
- altar table
- hiking boots
- candles
- tent kit
- cross
- rope
- knapsack
- hymnals

WORSHIP NOTES

Set up according to Sketch B. Place the altar table in the center with the cross and candles on it. Arrange the camping gear around the altar haphazardly. Have people sit in a circle and provide hymnals for them.

Try to make the room as comfortable as possible. "O Love That Will Not Let Me Go" is suggested as a responsive hymn. Sing one verse following each Scripture reading. The guided meditation suggested for use as a sermon can be found in the Appendix.

ORDER OF WORSHIP

GREETING

RESPONSIVE INVOCATION

L: We gather in God's name to be renewed.

P: We come looking for a safe, sacred space.

L: Lift us up on the wings of faith, Lord.

P: Lift us up with you to the mountaintop, so that we may commune with you and feel your presence.

ALL: Amen.

HYMN OF PRAISE: "God Hath Spoken by the Prophets"

OLD TESTAMENT: Exodus 24:12-18; II Kings 2:1-12*a*; Exodus 34:29-35

    Response: "O Love That Will Not Let Me Go," v. 1

RESPONSIVE PSALTER READING: Psalm 2:6-11; 50:1-6; 99

    Response: "O Love . . . ," v. 2

EPISTLE: II Peter 1:16-21; II Corinthians 4:3-6; II Corinthians 3:12–4:2

    Response: "O Love . . . ," v. 3

UNISON PRAYER

    The Transfiguration story is so hard for us to understand, God. Help us in our confusion and in our unbelief. As you did with Peter, take us along as you climb the peaks of faith. Bless us with visions of glory. Draw us near to you, that we may walk with you daily, as did Elijah. Give us the faith of Moses. And fill us with your Spirit. Walk with us also as we descend the mountain. Let us not despair when the glorious visions and closeness have cooled, but teach us to use the high points of faith to carry us through our moments of doubt. In Jesus' name, Amen.

    Response: "O Love . . . ," v. 4

PRAYERS OF THE PEOPLE with the Lord's Prayer

OFFERING with Doxology

HYMN OF PREPARATION: "When Morning Gilds the Skies"

GOSPEL: Matthew 17:1-9; Mark 9:2-9; Luke 9:28-36

MEDITATION

See the guided meditation in the Appendix.

AFFIRMATION OF FAITH

We believe in God—not a God who created the world and then stepped back, but a God who continues to claim us, call us, love us.

We believe in Jesus Christ, child of God, who descends the mountain with us to face times of high expectation and confusion.

We believe in the Holy Spirit, the power present at the Transfiguration. This same power works in and through us, transforming and uplifting us. Through us, this power transforms the world.

HYMN OF DEDICATION: "We Would See Jesus"

BENEDICTION

L: Friends of Jesus, we have been to the mountain, and our faith has been renewed. Go from this place carrying that message, to live as people who know they have been with the Messiah.

P: Amen.

POSTLUDE

SHROVE TUESDAY

Shrove Tuesday is precariously placed at the point of the Christian calendar immediately before the season of deepest penance. That it derives its name from the verb *shrive*, meaning to hear a confession, underscores its uniqueness. The common name Fat Tuesday refers to the Christian practice of eating doughnuts or pancakes in order to use the last bits of grease or leavening before Lent begins. The traditional Spanish name, Mardi Gras, refers to the carnivals which are part of the Shrove Tuesday tradition.

During the Lenten season people often speak of "giving up" something they enjoy as a symbol of self-discipline and penance. Thus, this is a time of final celebration and "luxury" before embarking upon the Lenten austerity.

This celebration may begin with coffee and doughnuts early in the morning, or with a pancake supper. Either way, emphasis should be placed on fun. We Christians are often better at penance than at festivity, so it could be helpful to provide games, fun hats, and other party items. Encourage people to wear colorful clothing, and decorate the room with bright streamers.

GATHER

- chalkboard and chalk
- colorful streamers
- doughnuts or pancakes and syrup
- piano
- games
- coffee
- tables
- hymnals
- party hats
- dish of flour

WORSHIP NOTES

Depending upon the available space, set up a room as close to the kitchen as possible, following Sketch C. Place a table at the center of the circle of chairs, with a cross in the center and candles on either side. Colorful fresh flowers may go beside each candle. To remind the worshipers that all we have, including our joys and our party foods, come from Christ, place the chalk and a small dish of flour in front of the cross. The flour symbolizes the elimination of leavening during Lent.

The chalkboard should be placed where everyone can see it without strain. Have a piano available if it will be needed for singing. Decorate the tables brightly and set them for the meal. They should be placed slightly away from the circle, but not so far that any separation of celebration from worship is suggested.

If possible, have a committee prepare the food before the service begins. Thus everyone can join in the circle, with as little division between worship and celebration as possible.

ORDER OF WORSHIP

GATHERING

A READING FROM THE GOSPEL: Matthew 9:14-17

CALL AND PRONOUNCEMENT

L: (This morning/Tonight) we join with Christians everywhere to celebrate the feast before Lenten fasting. As a resurrection people, we celebrate the presence of Jesus through the Holy Spirit. Ours is a God of plenty and of joy. Let us raise our voices in festive song!

HYMN: "Joyful, Joyful, We Adore Thee"

RESPONSIVE PSALTER: Psalm 100

TIME OF SHARING JOYS AND BLESSINGS
People are asked to share things that have given them joy during the past month. As they call them out, the leader writes them on the chalkboard. The group responds to each individual joy by saying, "Thanks be to God." This continues until the board is filled. Then all pause for a moment to appreciate the board filled with joy.

UNISON PRAYER OF THANKS

O God of Joy, we thank you for all the blessings that have been ours—for food, for home, for friends, for family, for You. May our celebration not end when the difficulties of life begin, but may we rest on your promise of plenty for all. Amen.

HYMN: "All Creatures of Our God and King"

Here the morning service ends and people move to the tables for doughnuts and coffee. In the evening service, a hymn-sing and games may follow the pancake supper.

ASH WEDNESDAY

The word *Lent*, from the old English *lencton*, means "spring." This period of Paschal preparation in the early spring of the year begins with Ash Wednesday and, in the Western church since the Nicean Council 325 C.E., extends for forty days.

In the ancient church, Lent served as a period of preparation for baptism on Easter Eve. For those under church discipline, it served as a period of public penance. The imposition of ashes is a carryover from this practice, and has extended to include all those who believe in the forgiveness of God. Fasting, sackcloth, and ashes have been the Judeo-Christian symbols of penance and mourning since Old Testament days.

Traditionally, the ashes are the product of burned palms from the previous Palm Sunday. The priest places them on the believer's forehead in the shape of a cross. However, in this service, our ashes come from burning our slips of paper. By imposing ashes upon ourselves, we uphold our belief that we acknowledge our own sins of commission and omission and that the absolution of these sins is a personal agreement between each of us and God.

The sacrificial meal which begins this Ash Wednesday service commemorates the traditional fasting of Lent. This type of discipline is symbolic of purification. Just as Jesus fasted for forty days in the desert, so we fast to draw nearer to God during this sacred time.

GATHER

- consommé
- basin of water
- matzo wafers
- white candles
- one large white candle
- fruit juice
- slips of paper and pencils
- burlap or white sheet
- pedestal (for candle)
- washcloth and
- tongs
- cauldron or bucket
- preburned palm ashes

WORSHIP NOTES

For this service, set the room according to Sketch C. Background music may be used, but silence is preferred. Use the burlap or white sheets as tablecloths, then place the white candles in a line down the center of the table. If possible, use enough candles to enable people to eat by candlelight.

In the center of the circle of chairs, set a pedestal with a large candle. Put slips of paper and pencils on each chair. On the floor beside the pedestal, place the cauldron or a small flame-resistant bucket containing the palm ashes. *Do not use wood ashes,* as they may cause toxic burns. Place the basin of water and washcloth on the floor opposite the pedestal.

Ask people to wait outside the room or in the sanctuary. At the appropriate time, invite them to begin singing the hymn and lead them to the table. Serve the consommé, crackers, and fruit juice as people gather. Then read the text from Matthew and proceed with the service.

After everyone has had ample time to finish the meal, silently lead them to the circle, light the candle, and sit down. Since there is a good deal of silence during this experience, it is good to be very comfortable with the quiet yourself. Move slowly and intentionally.

ORDER OF WORSHIP

GATHERING HYMN: "Sweet Hour of Prayer"

SACRIFICIAL MEAL

BLESSING in Unison

Just as we offer you thanks in times of plenty, O God, so make us grateful for this simple meal. May it serve to remind us of those for whom this would be a feast. Make us generous people. In the name of the One who cared for all, Amen.

MEDITATION

Read Matthew 4:1-11.

L: Now, I invite you to meditate on Jesus' time in the desert. Think of the times your faith has been tested and how you got through that period.

A few words may be said about fasting and sacrificial meals as symbols of purification.

PARTAKING OF THE MEAL in Silence

RITE OF THE ASHES

HYMN: "As I Survey the Wondrous Cross"

A TIME OF SELF-EXAMINATION

L: As we think about the time of Lent, our general focus is on a time 2,000 years ago. But tonight I want you to focus on temptation as Jesus was tempted. Our temptation may not be to control nature for our own desires or to have God at our beck and call. It may not be to rule the world or to amass great wealth. But in our own worlds and in our own ways, we are tempted to be completely self-sufficient, to need no one's help. We do have a tendency to think that God owes us something because we have been good and faithful; at times we do test God's love for us. We may laugh at the thought of ruling the world, though we are serious about ruling our own tiny corners.

Take a few minutes now to reflect upon those things that tempt you. In the barren places of your life, what temptations beset you? What holds you down? What things do you worship? What things do you need to release?

Write down the thing which most controls you—the thing about which you worry most, which you most seek to control, which you most would like to put out of your life. It is that thing you have never been able to give up to God. Write it down and look at it.

The leader goes to the center of the circle and ignites her/his own slip of paper in the flame of the candle. Use the tongs to hold the paper over the caldron while it turns, then drop the ashes into the cauldron.

L: As the paper burns, I release control. God will take charge. Together, we can do anything.

Invite each person to do the same. When each person has finished and the fire has ceased to burn, the leader dips a finger into the cauldron and puts a mark on her/his own hand.

L: These ashes remind us of the helplessness which comes of our need to control our lives.

The leader passes the cauldron around the circle, and each person dips into the cauldron until all have imposed ashes upon their own hands. The leader then takes the basin, dips the cloth into it, and washes the hand of the person next to her/him.

L: This water reminds us of the cleansing power of God's loving forgiveness. Nothing is beyond God's care.

As the basin goes around the circle, each person washes the ashes from the next person, proclaiming the same. When this has been done all around the circle, the leader shall say:

L: Christ gave his life to teach us the Way. Be released from any temptation that binds you.

HYMN: "Amazing Grace"

BENEDICTION

Our Christ has been with us tonight. He who withstood the temptations in the desert goes with us through the next forty days of testing and purification. Go now, knowing that he fills you with strength while he leads the way. Amen.

(*All leave in silence*)

PALM SUNDAY

I n fourth-century Jerusalem, Christians met on the Mount of Olives and carried branches while escorting the bishop into the city. This commemorated the event of Jesus' ride into Jerusalem before his crucifixion. The general spread of this and similar traditions gave this day its name. *Hosanna*, literally a cry for help—"God save us"—was first used in the Passover ritual.

When the church firmly established the times of celebration for the Feast of the Resurrection, it also separated the events of the passion, which led up to and included the crucifixion. Thus, Holy Week, beginning with Palm Sunday, commemorates all the events leading up to Jesus' passion, death, and resurrection.

GATHER

- palm branches
- altar
- tape
- cross
- a small burro figure
- candles
- burlap

WORSHIP NOTES

Set up according to Sketch A. On the altar, lay criss-cross palm branches and place the cross and candles on them. If a small burro figurine is available, place it in the center of the altar in front of the cross. If such a figure is not available, cut a piece of burlap and place it on the altar to serve as a reminder of the humble character of Jesus' glorious ride.

Tape palm branches to the ends of the pews or give one to each worshiper as she/he enters the sanctuary. They will take these home with them at the end of the service as a reminder of the tension between glory and passion in the week ahead.

The emphasis today is twofold. Glory is apparent: Palm Sunday is the day we celebrate Jesus' exultant ride into Jerusalem. Celebration and praise are the theme of the day. Included with this motif, though, is the fickleness of the crowd. Within the space of one week of the Christian calendar, we remember Jesus' glory, servanthood, torment, death, and triumphant resurrection. It can make people's heads spin!

Each part is important and deserves its time. This service is devoted to Palm Sunday, rather than to Passion Sunday. Effort has been taken, however, to include the foreshadowing of events to come.

Special music may be added after the prayers or after the sermon. We suggest "The Palms," "Ride on, King Jesus," or "Tell Me the Stories of Jesus." The Scriptures for the day were chosen from the lection.

ORDER OF WORSHIP

GATHERING

PRELUDE

INTROIT: "Prepare Ye the Way of the Lord"

CALL TO WORSHIP

L: Grab your palm branches and come running!

P: Lay your coats upon the ground.

L: The Prince of Peace is coming.

P: See how he rides like a king!

L: Glory is all around him,

P: Though he borrowed a donkey for the ride.

L: Grab your palm branches and come running!

P: Lay your coats upon the ground.

HYMN: "Hosanna, Loud Hosanna!"

OLD TESTAMENT: Isaiah 50:4-9*a*

LITANY OF PRAISE: Psalm 118:19-29

L: Open to me the door of the Temple and I will go in and give thanks. This is God's holy door; only the righteous can come in. I give you thanks, Holy One, because you heard me, because you strengthened me and held me up.

P: Give thanks to our Creator, who is good and whose love is eternal.

L: The stone which the builders thought worthless turned out to be the most important of all. God did this, and what a wonderful sight it is! This is the day of Divine Success. Let us celebrate and be happy! Redeem us and give us success, O Divine Guide.

P: Give thanks to our Creator, who is good and whose love is eternal.

L: May God bless the One who comes in the name of the Creator! From the Temple, we bless you. The Creator is God, who has been good to us.

P: Give thanks to our Creator, who is good and whose love is eternal.

L: With branches in your hands, begin the festival and march around the altar.

P: You are my God, and I give you thanks; I will proclaim your greatness.

ALL: Give thanks to our Creator, who is good and whose love is eternal. Amen.

PRAYERS OF THE PEOPLE with the Lord's Prayer

EPISTLE: Philippians 2:5-11

OFFERTORY with the Doxology

HYMN OF PREPARATION: "Rejoice, Ye Pure in Heart"

GOSPEL: Matthew 21:1-11; Mark 11:1-11; Luke 19:28-40

SERMON

Palm Sunday is an anomaly. This is not the time of final triumph. The same crowds which laud Jesus now will turn on him soon. The same people who lay their coats down for him to ride across will strip the clothes from his back later in order to lash and spit on him. Jesus is not fooled. He knows what is in people's hearts. But the triumphal entry is a necessary part of the process.

Crowds still are fickle. They tickertape a hero, then try to get the "dirt" on her/him later. Rumors and devious talk have created many a feud and much pain.

Concentrate on the love and service Jesus offered to the people around him, and on his insight into human nature.

PRAYER OF DEDICATION
O Great Lover of the world, what must it require to give up your own child? How must it feel when people praise him to his face and condemn him behind his back? We sit here and wave our palm branches, but in our minds we wonder, Where would we have been when Jesus entered Jerusalem? Would we have joined the crowds to ask for healing, then turned our backs to yell, "Crucify him!" Could we have stood solidly against our friends and family, or would we have joined the jeering masses?

O Gracious Creator, we want to be faithful. Our wills are strong and our commitment is sure. We dedicate our lives to you now. Make us steadfast wise Christians, capable of standing against popular opinion, able to love without regard to reward, able to serve without concern for gain. We want to be trustworthy people who wave their palm branches consistently to the glory of Christ—our redeemer, healer, friend. Amen.

HYMN OF DEDICATION: "Lord, I Want to Be a Christian"

BENEDICTION
L: Go forth and remember whom you have praised here. Remember through the supper, remember through the foot washing, remember through the trials, the agony, the death. Let that memory give you hope through the days ahead.

P: Amen.

POSTLUDE

MAUNDY (HOLY) THURSDAY

Holy Thursday, also called Maundy Thursday, from the Latin *mandatum*, meaning "command", is the day we remember Jesus' last meal with the twelve. It was on this day that Jesus gathered his disciples together in the upper room, ate with them, and then washed their feet (John 13). During the washing, Jesus gave them the command to love one another. Today's celebration, though somber, is also one of love. The extreme cost of love, which Jesus was willing to pay, underscores the tender solemnity of this worship service.

Christians at the beginning of our faith history remembered this occasion with an ordinary meal. It was only later that the Lord's Supper was separated from the common meal. The original meal in the upper room was a true dining together, while Jesus shared his last words, his last bit of teaching. Thus, the Agape Meal, or feast of love, should be celebrated with a spirit that closely resembles a dinner among friends or family. If the organist wishes to participate fully, recorded music may provide the worshipful background.

Because of the sensitivity of foot washing, we have substituted hand washing. This also ties in with the hand washing of Ash Wednesday at the beginning of Lent. The celebrant may use a basin and towel to more closely resemble Jesus' act.

GATHER

- grape juice
- fresh fruit (cut in wedges)
- napkins
- paper plates
- a variety of crackers
- paper cups
- tablecloths
- a loaf of bread (unsliced)
- candles
- chalice
- communion linens
- towel and basin

WORSHIP NOTES

The set-up for this service should resemble Sketch C. The table service should be all white, with the candles lined down the center of the table. A tape recorder or other simple means could supply background music.

Place the elements for the Eucharist at the center of the head table, covered by the communion linens. The basin and towel may be placed on either side of the elements. Finally, place the food evenly over the tables in a way that resembles a traditional meal.

Since this service centers around the Holy Meal, the entire service will take place with the people gathered around the table. Eucharist should be done by intinction.

Have the people wait in the sanctuary or somewhere away from the room where the service will take place. Keep that area closed off so that no one wanders in. At time to begin, the leader should read from Jeremiah, announce that the table is set, and invite the people to enter the "upper room."

ORDER OF WORSHIP

GATHERING

PROCLAMATION: Jeremiah 31:31-34

PROCESSION TO THE UPPER ROOM

INVITATION AND PRAYER: Hebrews 10:16-25

HYMN OF RESPONSE: "Here, O My Lord, I See Thee Face to Face"

SHARING OF THE AGAPE FEAST

HYMN OF DEDICATION: "For the Bread Which Thou Hast Broken"

LORD'S SUPPER: Luke 22:7-20
Great Thanksgiving. Denominational liturgy may be used.

Great God, we have heard again the story of Jesus' meal with the twelve. There he took the ordinary staples of life—bread and wine— and made them into an extraordinary feast. You have invited us to remember and celebrate that sacramental meal. With power and blessing, may your Spirit touch these elements and anoint us with grace. In the name of the One who calls us here, Amen.

Breaking of the Bread

Sharing of the Cup

PRAYER OF THANKS

O Lord, it is at your table that we remember you most. As we partake of these elements, fill us not only with their substance, but also with your Spirit. As we gather here to reenact the meal you shared with the original disciples, remind us of your presence with us. And recommit us to your mission. In your name we pray. Amen.

RITUAL OF HAND WASHING: John 13:1-17

HYMN: "What Wondrous Love Is This?"

GETHSEMANE STORY: Matthew 26:36-46

HYMN: "Go to Dark Gethsemane"

BLESSING

L: We have been the guests of the Christ. He has shared his food.

P: He has shared his life.

L: He has cleansed our bodies.

P: He has cleansed our souls.

L: We have learned of commitment.

P: We have learned of love.

ALL: Bless us, O Christ, in the days to come. As we pass through horrible death to the sunrise of your resurrection, fill us with your hope and rekindle in us your wondrous love for all people everywhere. Lift us up with your grace and lead us on. Amen.

BENEDICTION HYMN: "God Be with You 'Til We Meet Again"

L: Go in peace, knowing that you have communed with our Lord.

GOOD FRIDAY

Although the true origin of the term *Good Friday* is obscure, many traditions exist. Some believe it to be a derivation of "God Friday"; others think it emphasizes the importance of what Christ accomplished through crucifixion. Whatever the meaning, the act of love acted out on that day remains indisputable.

Tenebrae is the Latin word for "darkness." Traditionally, services of public chanting and psalter vigils were common on Holy Thursday, Friday, and Saturday. As each of fourteen psalms was read, a candle was extinguished. The fifteenth candle, which continued to burn, was then placed behind the altar.

In the Roman world, Christians spent forty hours of fasting and vigil in remembrance of Christ's time in the grave. The fasting did not end until the glorious dawn of Easter morning.

This Service of Scripture and Hymn is an alternative to the traditional Seven Last Words format. While incorporating the tenebrae ritual, it also allows worshipers to meditate on the crucifixion story as recorded in the Gospel of John. As the candles are extinguished, we follow Jesus' path of increasing darkness from betrayal to grave.

GATHER

- 14 white candles
- 2 tenebrae candelabra
- hammer
- dark cloth
- a board with nails slightly pounded into it
- altar
- cross
- 2 altar candles

WORSHIP NOTES

Set up according to Sketch A. Drape the dark cloth over the altar cross. Place the candelabra on either side of the altar. Light all fourteen candles, plus the two altar candles.

Worshipers enter a lighted sanctuary. The ceiling lights should be extinguished during the Words of Preparation. Leave only enough light for reading.

Following the Words of Preparation, remind people of the significance of Good Friday and the darkness of the crucifixion. Then proceed with the first Scripture. Liturgists may be invited to read the Scriptures, or the leader may read all seven. There should be as little confusion and disruption of the service as possible. After each Scripture lesson is read, the congregation will immediately begin the hymn. While the hymn is being sung, acolytes will extinguish the pair of candles farthest from the altar on each of the candelabra. Allow the altar candles to burn.

Beginning with the reading of Lesson 5 and continuing through the reading of Lesson 6, someone might pound a series of nails into a board located in an area out of sight of the sanctuary. This should be audible, but not diversionary. The hammering ceases as the congregation sings "What Wondrous Love Is This."

ORDER OF WORSHIP

A SERVICE OF SCRIPTURE AND SACRED SONG

PRELUDE

LIGHTING OF THE CANDLES

WORDS OF PREPARATION

L: A world that could not understand the power of Love turned upon the one for whom they had waited for so many generations. They tortured and killed the One who could save them. So that we do not forget, let us read the story once again.

P: **So that we do not forget, so that we never forget what the power of Love can do, we will hear the story again. May it increase our understanding.**

ALL: Amen.

LESSON 1: John 18:1-22—JUDAS BETRAYS JESUS
> Hymn: "'Tis Midnight, and on Olive's Brow"
> *Extinguishing of the first candles.*

LESSON 2: John 18:12-14, 19-24—TRIAL WITH CAIAPHAS
> Hymn: "O Love Divine, What Hast Thou Done?"
> *Extinguishing of the second candles.*

LESSON 3: John 18:25-27—PETER DENIES JESUS
> Hymn: "Ah, Holy Jesus"

PRAYER OF CONFESSION in Unison
> **How many times we have denied you, O Christ! When we do not notice the hungry and the homeless, when we fail to hear the cries of loneliness, when we walk past the victim en route to our own safety, the cock crows also in our lives, and we are as guilty as Peter. Forgive us, O Christ. Amen.**

WORDS OF ASSURANCE
> Be aware that our denials cannot stop the love of Jesus. Amen.

Extinguishing of the third candles

LESSON 4: John 18:28–19:16—TRIAL WITH PILATE
> Hymn: "O Sacred Head, Now Wounded"
> *Extinguishing of the fourth candles*

LESSON 5: John 19:17-30—CRUCIFIXION
> Hymn: "Were You There When They Crucified My Lord?"
> *Extinguishing of the fifth candles*

LESSON 6: John 19:31-37—JESUS' DEATH PROVEN
> Hymn: "When the Storms of Life Are Raging"
> *Extinguishing of the sixth candles*

LESSON 7: John 19:38-42—BURIAL OF JESUS
> Hymn: "Let All Mortal Flesh Keep Silence"
> *Extinguishing of the seventh candles*

BENEDICTION: John 3:16

POSTLUDE

All leave the sanctuary in silence.

EASTER VIGIL

All through Christian history, the Feast of the Resurrection has been the great event of the religious year, giving a whole new aspect to Passover. As the church grew, however, the only point of agreement between East and West was their determination that Easter should never fall on the same day as Passover. Thus, East and West avoid Passover—and very often each other!—in their celebrative days. The current formula for setting the time of Easter is a compromise reached in Nicaea in 325 C.E.: the first Sunday after the full moon after the equinox, still based on the Jewish season of Passover.

Traditionally, all the events of Jesus' passion were celebrated with a unified Paschal service; after Constantine, separate services were held. Christians observed Easter with the Lord's Supper, so Easter Eve was a favorite time for baptism, since only initiated (baptized) Christians could commune. The irony came later in the Middle Ages, when the mass became so clerical that worshipers could not understand the service. As a result, participation dropped so radically that when the Fourth Lateran Council met in 1215 C.E., it required that the faithful receive Communion once a year on Easter, rather than merely observing as the priest partook.

GATHER

- communion elements   • black drape cloth   • white drape cloth
- altar table   • altar cross   • fresh flowers
- baptismal font or bowl with water   • Paschal (white) candle

WORSHIP NOTES

Set up the sanctuary according to Sketch A, or the social hall according to Sketch B. The altar should be empty and covered with the black cloth at the beginning of the service. The altar cross and candle should be stored somewhere near, but out of sight. When people come in, give each one a fresh-cut flower.

As the prelude is played, two people should rush to the altar, remove the black cloth, fold it, then replace it with the white cloth, and place the cross and candle on the altar. When the altar has been set, the same two, or two others, bring the Communion elements (loaf and chalice) to the altar and place them in front of the cross. Then the leader lights the Paschal candle and exclaims, "Christ is risen!" With this, the order of worship begins. During the first hymn, the worshipers come forward and place their flowers on the altar.

The order of worship is adapted from those in the ante-Nicene period (100–325 C.E.), the first formal Christian order of worship. The Great Thanksgiving prayer may be used prior to Communion, which should be by intinction. The meditation, "Letter to a Sister," is included in the Appendix. The Scripture readings were selected from the lection choices. Only the Gospel readings vary by year A, B, and C. An adaptation of this service for sunrise follows.

ORDER OF WORSHIP

SYNAXIS ("meeting")

GREETING AND RESPONSE

L: Christ is Risen!

P: Christ is Risen, indeed!

ALL: Praise be to God!

SCRIPTURE: (select from the texts for the Vigil—Gen. 1:1–2:2, 7:1-5, 11-18; 8:6-18, 9:8-13, 22:1-18; Exod. 14:10–15:1; Isa. 54:5-14, 55:1-11; Bar. 3:9-15, 32; 4:4; Ezra 36:24-28, 37:1-14; Zeph. 3:14-20)

HYMN: "Low in the Grave He Lay"

EPISTLE: (A, B, and C—Rom. 6:3-11)

PSALM in Unison: Psalm 98

GOSPEL: (Matt. 28:1-10; Mark 16:1-8; Luke 24:1-12)

HYMN: "Now the Green Blade Riseth"

SERMON: "Letter to a Sister" *(see Appendix)*

PRAYERS

O God of the Impossible, rekindle our hopes. Forgive our doubt. Remove the suspicion that blinds our eyes to your miraculous ways. Remind us anew that the separation between life and death is not so extreme. Jesus has shown us the truth. Life is a journey which does not end when our body ceases to act. Life goes on and on and on—forever. Amen.

At this time, the ancient church would have excused the unbaptized Christians. The leader may mark this by renewal of baptism, see "Baptism of Our Lord" chapter.

EUCHARIST ("thanks giving")

GREETINGS AND RESPONSE

L: By whose authority are you here?

P: We are the ones Christ called friends.

L: What path do you follow?

P: By the grace of God, we follow the Way of the Risen Christ.

L: Do you live in harmony with the covenant community, your neighbors, the world?

P: We try to do as our leader taught us. There are times, when we have fallen short of our calling. Those things we confess now before God . . . (*moments of silence*).

L: God hears our confession and shows us mercy. Come now, you are welcome at the table of Christ.

KISS OF PEACE

Greet one another, saying, "The Peace of Christ be with you."

OFFERTORY

If no offering is to be taken at this service, sing a communion hymn here.

GREAT PRAYER with the Lord's Prayer

L: Before the world, God was, making sense of the void, separating night from day, and ordering creation. When people threatened to bring back the confusion, God sent flood waters and prophets. When the world seemed hopelessly disheveled, God sent Jesus Christ. In his life, death, and resurrection, the world learned peace and wholeness, healing and righteousness.

On the night he was to be turned over to his powers of death, Jesus gathered around him those whom he had called. He told them of the things to come. He broke ordinary bread and said, "This is my body." He poured wine and said, "This is my blood." They ate and drank of these as he told them to do, saying, "When you do this, remember me."

Send, O Creator, the power of the Holy Spirit on this bread and on this cup. Bless them and all who partake of them, that we may partake with you of Life Eternal. Amen.

P: Our Father, who art in heaven . . .

FRACTION (*breaking of the bread*)

COMMUNION (*distribution of the elements*)

DISMISSAL

L: We have gone with Mary to the empty tomb. The Master has spoken to us. We have seen with our own eyes what we thought was impossible, and we claim it for ourselves. Go now into the world of pain and death, spreading the hope of Eternal Life. You are called to be the Resurrection People. Amen.

P: Amen.

HYMN: "O Mary, Don't You Weep"

POSTLUDE

EASTER SUNRISE SERVICE

ORDER OF WORSHIP

GATHERING

GREETING AND RESPONSE

L: By whose authority are you here?

P: We are the ones Christ called friends.

L: What path do you follow?

P: By the grace of God, we follow the Way of the Risen Christ.

L: Christ is Risen!

P: Christ is Risen indeed!

ALL: Praise be to God!

HYMN: "Low in the Grave He Lay"

SCRIPTURE

Choose about three Scripture texts, using the lections for the morning. See the Easter Vigil section.

HYMN: "He Lives!"

SERMON: "Letter to a Sister" *(see Appendix)*

PRAYERS

O God of the impossible, rekindle our hopes. Forgive our doubt. Remove the suspicion that blinds our eyes to your miraculous way. Remind us anew that the separation between life and death is not so extreme. Jesus has shown us the truth. Life is a journey which does not end when our body ceases to act. Life goes on and on and on— forever. Amen.

KISS OF PEACE

Greet one another, saying, "The Peace of Christ be with you."

GREAT PRAYER with the Lord's Prayer

HYMN: "O Mary, Don't You Weep"

DISMISSAL

L: We have gone with Mary to the empty tomb. The Master has spoken to us. We have seen with our own eyes what is possible. And we claim it for ourselves. Go now into the world of pain and death, spreading the hope of Eternal Life. You are called to be the Resurrection People. Amen.

P: Amen.

ASCENSION DAY

This final appearance of Christ to his followers is celebrated forty days after Easter's resurrection celebration. It was this magnificent scene that gave the motivation the followers needed for their future ministry. It supplies the preparation and foreshadowing for Pentecost and the birth of the church. The scene probably took place on the Mount of Olives, overlooking Jerusalem.

The closest such occurrence in the Old Testament is the translation of Enoch or the assumption of Elijah. In the New Testament, Matthew does not mention the Ascension, and Mark's mention is contained in a questionable addition to the text. John refers to the event, but includes no narrative. Luke mentions the Ascension twice. In the Gospel, it follows the resurrection, unifying the two events. Acts 1:13 places the Ascension forty days afterward, symbolizing the completion of Jesus' mission on earth. From the fourth century through the present, this day generally has been accepted as an important part of the Christian year.

The mood on this day is celebrative. It commemorates the rising of Christ in his resurrected body from earth to heaven. Emphasis should be placed on the sequence: Christ does not pass directly to heaven, but first passes through suffering and death. This day is filled with the rejoicing of a Resurrection People who are seeing their leader's promises, and their own dreams, come true before their own eyes. Like Easter, this is a true commemoration of the power of life.

GATHER

- white drape cloth
- altar
- cross
- 1 white pillar candle
- white votive candles and holders
- long matches
- 3 readers

WORSHIP NOTES

Set up according to Sketch B, with the altar as part of the circle, rather than in the middle. (If this service is used as morning worship on the Sunday nearest to Ascension Day, set up in the sanctuary according to Sketch A.) On the altar, place the cross, the white pillar candle, and the white cloth. Arrange the cloth so that it looks as if it has fallen from the ceiling. Then place six, nine, or twelve votive candles around the cloth or in front of the cross. If they are in holders, there will be no danger of fire.

Although this is a day of high celebration, the tone should be simple and straightforward. Jesus told the disciples about the Ascension, but they were amazed, an amazement which still exists in our own culture, even after 2,000 years. Resurrection is, however, basic to our faith. The cloth and the candle are reminders of this, while the cross reminds us of the suffering and death before the Ascension. Both events are part of our faith heritage. The candle should also remind people that the time of Ascension is still a time of hope. Resolution does not come until the descent of the Holy Spirit at Pentecost. The suggested Order of Worship contains all the parts of a more formal Sunday service. If used on Ascension Day itself, allow some flexibility in the service. The prayers of the people should be done informally.

At the beginning of the service, immediately following the prelude, selected individuals should read the story of each of Jesus' appearances to his followers. After each reading, the person will light one-third of the votive candles, until all the Scriptures are read and all the candles are lighted. The leader should read the Ascension verses, then light the white pillar candle while beginning the call to worship: "From the cross to the garden . . ."

ORDER OF WORSHIP

PRELUDE

READING OF THE WORD AND LIGHTING OF THE CANDLES

Readers: Mark 16:9-11; Mark 16:12-13; Mark 16:14-18

Leader: Mark 16:19-20

CALL TO WORSHIP

L: From the cross to the garden, from Emmaus to Ascension, Christ rises victorious over death.

P: **The life that God has shared is reunited now: Christ and God are one.**

L: We follow, watching in wonder these events of so long ago.

P: **We watch, and our faith is strengthened each time the tale is retold.**

L: People of God, your Christ has risen!

P: **Alleluia! Christ is Lord!**

OPENING HYMN: "All Hail the Power of Jesus' Name"

EPISTLE: Acts 1:1-11

RESPONSIVE ACT OF PRAISE: Psalm 47

UNISON PRAYER

**O God, we feel so close to you on days of glory when your power
and magnificence are felt throughout the church. Build our faith, that
we too may rise on wings of eagles, so that we may soar in your vision
and know a unity with you. Because of Jesus Christ, we know that life
reigns over death, that we too will rise again on that day when our
bodies give up breath. Teach us now, though, God. Bless us with your
assurance that we may rest in the sure knowledge that life is not so
separate, nor death so final, that we ever need to be afraid. In the
name of the Ascended One, Amen.**

PRAYERS OF THE PEOPLE with the Lord's Prayer

HYMN OF PREPARATION: "Ask Me What Great Thing I Know"

GOSPEL: Luke 24:46-53

SERMON

*As the witnesses stand and watch, they see in real form what Christ had told
them would happen. Truth is often hard to take in; even in our world we often
forget that death is not the final word. It is easy to allow hopelessness to overtake us when someone we love dies. Our grief blinds us to Christ's promises.
The Spirit is yet to come, but Christ has proved the power of life over death. You
may want to preach, or merely offer this as a time of reflection (verbal or silent)
on the impact of this Ascension story on the people gathered for this service—the
modern witnesses.*

AFFIRMATION OF FAITH

**We believe in God, who formed the worlds and breathed life into
the universe.**

**We believe in Jesus, God present in human form: our example,
teacher, friend. Christ gave his love through his great love for humanity. On the third day after death, Christ rose again to the world to commune with Mary and those who had been with him.**

**After he had prepared the believers for their mission, he ascended
into the heavens. He was reunited fully with God.**

**We believe in the Spirit as God's presence with us for guidance and
strength.**

In life and in death, in triumph and in trial, God is always with us. Praise be to God! Amen.

HYMN OF DEDICATION: "Thine Be the Glory"

BENEDICTION

L: We too are witnesses to the great power of love over death.

P: We too await the Spirit's descent.

L: And the mystery is this: Death has been put away and life springs eternal. For we are raised with Christ.

P: Praise be to God!

POSTLUDE

PENTECOST

During Jesus' final appearance, he promised the faithful that he would send One who would lead them. Pentecost marks the anointing of the disciples with the Spirit and with fire. *Penta* indicates "five"; technically, Pentecost (Whitsunday, or White Sunday, in the Church of England) is celebrated fifty days after Easter and completes the Paschal season. Originally, this was the time of the Jewish pilgrim festival Shabuoth, the Festival of Weeks described in Leviticus 23:15-21. This holiday commemorated the ingathering of wheat and God's giving of the decalogue. Shabuoth began fifty days after the first day of Passover and concluded with the day of Pentecost. Christians adapted this celebration to their own ends and thus celebrate the birthday of the church on Pentecost, fifty days after Easter.

Such an enormous gathering of believers came together in the miraculous harmony of the Spirit on that first Pentecost that it has been observed from the beginning, and has been a major feast day from at least the third century. Fasting was set aside, and there was no kneeling during public prayer.

GATHER

- 7 red candles of various heights (pillar candles are best)
- colorful banners   • communion elements
- cassette recordings of different languages (optional)
- incense (preferably frankincense) in either cones or sticks

WORSHIP NOTES

Set up according to Sketch A or B, depending upon the size of the group and the level of intimacy and informality desired. Colorful banners may be created to list the gifts of the Spirit, depict the Spirit's flame, and so on. In addition to the cross, the altar should be filled with red candles in multiples of seven. Pillar candles are easier to use; they burn longer and do not drip.

The optimum ritual would have people read the Scriptures in various languages. If this is impossible, the miracle of cross-cultural communication present at Pentecost can be experienced through the use of audiotapes. Tapes designed to teach language may be the most readily available and can be found in most public libraries. All these may be used simultaneously following the processional chant, or if a specific message is to be conveyed, they may be used singly and interpreted. Efforts should be made to ensure that the languages represent as wide a global spectrum as possible—East, West, South, North. It is also possible to select a single word such as *peace* and recite it in different languages, or to create a banner using the forms of this word.

Because of the historicity of this feast day, we have chosen to use the basic form of worship from the post-Nicene period (325–604 C.E.). This reflects the time when the service was no longer divided at the point of Communion; baptized and unbaptized believers worshiped together throughout the service.

Intinction is the preferred mode of Communion, both because of its simplicity and because of its use of the common cup. In a sanctuary setting, have the people come to the altar to be served by the celebrant. In a social-room setting, start the bread and the chalice with one person in the circle, then have each person serve the next person, saying, "The body and blood of Jesus Christ, Amen."

The incense may stay on the altar or be passed among the people. This ritual symbolized the cleansing of the worshipers and the room, which helped to create sacred space.

ORDER OF WORSHIP

INTRODUCTORY RITES

GATHERING AND ENTRANCE

PROCESSIONAL CHANT: "Let It Breathe on Me," "Pass It On," or "Spirit"

Leader enters and the candles are lighted.

GREETING

L: Come, gather in this place of blessing.

P: We come, seeking the leading of the Spirit.

L: Our ancestors gathered before us: Peter and Mary, Paul and Lydia, Timothy and Priscilla, and all the disciples.

P: We come, like them, opening ourselves to this One, whose coming Christ has promised.

ALL: All is ready. Let us worship.

CENSING *Light the incense*

LITANY WITH KYRIE

L: Spirit of Wisdom and Truth, on this day you came among the people and blessed them with the gifts of wisdom, understanding, counsel, fortitude, knowledge, faithfulness, and fear of God. Out of that band of people, you created the world church. We pray now for your leading:

L: For the church in Africa, may it stand strong as a beacon of hope and love amidst division, racism, and the struggle for independence.

P: Be a source of wisdom in Africa. Heal us and make us one.

L: For the church in Asia, may it continue to grow as it ministers to poverty, change, and development.

P: Be a source of wisdom in Asia. Heal us and make us one.

L: For the church in Europe and Australia, may it give calm to a world of decaying systems and changing times.

P: Be a source of wisdom in Europe and Australia. Heal us and make us one.

L: For the church in South and Central America, may it continue to be a strong voice of commitment for the people.

P: Be a source of wisdom in South and Central America. Heal us and make us one.

L: For the church in North America, may it challenge all arrogance and call for humble devotion to the needs of the meek.

P: Be a source of wisdom in North America. Heal us and make us one.

ALL: O God of All Peoples, forgive our ignorance and apathy. Purify us from our sin: what we have done, what we have failed to do. Purify us and make us one.

KYRIE

L: Lord, have mercy upon us.

P: Lord, have mercy upon us.

L: Christ, have mercy upon us.

P: Christ, have mercy upon us.

ALL: Lord, have mercy upon us,

And give us peace. Amen.

HYMN: "Help Us Accept Each Other"

SYNAXIS

OLD TESTAMENT: (Isa. 44:1-8; Ezra 37:1-4; Gen. 11:1-9)

PSALM in Unison: Psalm 104:24-34

EPISTLE: Acts 2:1-13

HYMN: "Spirit of God, Descend Upon My Heart"

GOSPEL: (John 20:19-23; John 15:26-27, 16:4b-15; John 14:8-17, 25-27)

HYMN: "Spirit of the Living God, Fall Afresh on Me"

SERMON

It is possible to read the Epistle here and preach Peter's message as it was delivered to the first gathering of the church (see Appendix). If the Epistle is used as marked, use this time to concentrate on the end results of the divisions we have in our present world. As creation matures, there is less and less room for isolation and discord. Our world community needs harmony. The worldwide church can be a wellspring of this peaceful diversity.

PRAYERS in Unison

As the people of the resurrection, O God, we stand united by your call. The life of Christ has redeemed us. The blessing of the Spirit has empowered us. Touch our community and heal our wounded who need your special touch. Lead the universal Church, in its ministry with the world. Inspire us to live in peace with our next-door neighbors and our neighbors around the world. Help us create a world in which all may eat, have shelter and gainful employment, a community of support. Challenge us to work for your kingdom, O Great Creator of the universe. Make us wise stewards, patient mediators, empathic friends and lovers, faithful followers of your Way. In Christ's name, Amen.

EUCHARIST

LORD'S PRAYER in Unison

PREPARATORY PRAYER BEFORE COMMUNION

Great Thanksgiving

(*Denominational prayers may be substituted.*)

L: From the void, O God, you created the universe with diversity, with color, with harmony. When division threatened to overtake the world, you sent cleansing flood waters until the rainbow appeared, proclaiming a new covenant. Since that time, prophets and healers have cleansed the earth and reminded the people of your Way.

When division threatened the world again, you sent Christ to teach, to heal, to show the way. On the night he would be betrayed, he gathered his friends around him for a common meal. He explained his death and resurrection and taught them to carry on his mission. After he left them, he sent the Spirit to guide, direct, and lead them.

Send, O God, the power of that same Spirit upon these elements of bread and wine, that in the partaking of these common foods, we may be reminded of the uncommon words of Christ and follow the path of the Spirit's leading. Amen.

BLESSING OF THE PEOPLE

L: You who live in harmony with your neighbors, who follow the way of Christ, who live in accordance with the Spirit's teaching, are called of God to be co-creators in the Plan of the Ages. You are called into the ministry of Christ, to share love and empathic concern wherever it is needed.

As Christ gathered his friends in the first upper room, Christ bids you to come now. Come, share the feast.

SHARING OF THE ELEMENTS

POST-COMMUNION PRAYERS in Unison

We have been with you at your table, O Christ. We have eaten of your food and tasted your wine. We offer you our thanks and praise— a people revived by your love. Amen.

CONCLUDING RITES

PRIESTLY BLESSING

L: O Source of our being, go with your people as they leave this place. Fill them with the sure knowledge that they carry your Spirit within them. Let all that they do and all that they are reflect your love and inspiration, to the end that the world will be one in union with you. In the name of the Triune God,

ALL: Amen.

HYMN: "Sweet, Sweet Spirit"

DISMISSAL

CHRISTIAN UNITY GATHERING

Oikoumené is a Greek word meaning "inhabited earth." Thus, ecumenism focuses on the Christian faith and its study and practice all over the world. In the middle of this century, the Consultation on Church Unity (COCU) was born from the dialogue and proposal issued by Presbyterian Stated Clerk Eugene Carson Blake and Episcopal Bishop James Pike. The Disciples of Christ expressed strong interest, and the movement has grown into an organization responsible for bringing various denominations together for dialogue, worship, mission, and growth.

The Week of Christian Unity is devoted to that purpose. During this week, churches have the opportunity to join with Christians from other traditions for worship, prayer, study, and fellowship. This service begins that week of *oikoumené*.

GATHER

- burlap or other material
- crosses from various denominations
- liturgists and clergy from different churches in the community
- altar candles
- liquid embroidery paint or felt
- altar
- cross

WORSHIP NOTES

Depending upon the size of the group, set up either in the sanctuary, following Sketch A, or in a social room, following Sketch B. Place an altar in the center of the worship space and place a cross and candles on it. All Christians use the cross as their primary symbol, but denominations often adapt it for their own use. A group in the church could make a banner containing the crosses of as many denominations as possible, or each congregation could be invited to bring the flag or cross of its own denomination. If this is done, make a special time in the service for representatives of each denomination to identify their own cross or flag and comment about it, or mention one thing that is special about their tradition.

To make this service as ecumenical as possible, plan it with members of the other denominations in the area and/or invite other churches to participate in the service. To facilitate this, the service might best be held on an afternoon or evening.

Since this service does not fall on a consistent day of the Christian calendar, we have chosen Scripture which deals with the topic of the service.

ORDER OF WORSHIP

GATHERING

PRELUDE

GREETING

CALL TO WORSHIP

L: Today is the day we concentrate on our similarities with other Christians.

P: Today we celebrate God's love, poured out on all people.

L: Today we affirm our differences.

P: Today we are united across denominational lines.

L: With joy, let us come from all over the earth to worship God, the Creator of variety.

P: With joy, let us praise God, whose love is given to all.

HYMN OF PRAISE: "Lift Every Voice and Sing"

OLD TESTAMENT: Genesis 9:12-17

PRAYER OF CONFESSION

Today, O God, we gather together to worship you. But our hearts are sad as we recall the ways we divide ourselves from one another— by clothes, skin color, income, politics. We are sorry that we see differences as problems, when you see variety as opportunity. Teach us, Creator God, how to leave petty jealousy of others' success behind and learn to build up one another. In that way, may we learn to work harmoniously for your good, rather than as soloists for our own good. In the name of Jesus who unites us all, Amen.

WORDS OF ASSURANCE

Together, we stand as a people forgiven and unified under the care and protection of one God.

ANTHEM (*optional*)

TIME OF SHARING *Representatives of each church speak—optional.*

EPISTLE: Colossians 3:11-17

PRAYERS OF THE PEOPLE with the Lord's Prayer

OFFERING with Doxology (*optional*)

HYMN OF PREPARATION: "We Are One in the Spirit"

GOSPEL: Mark 3:31-35

SERMON

The sermon could focus on what unites us—doing God's work. Not everyone has the same skill or talent or viewpoint, but everyone's skill or talent or viewpoint should be used for the common good. An evening ecumenical service might be exciting! We have common roots: God's covenant people from Noah's story. Let's use this service to concentrate on things that unite, rather than divide us.

RESPONSE AFTER SERMON (*Alternative: Apostles' Creed*)

I believe in the world, God's created order, operating with God's full participation and attention. I am part of this created order.

I believe in the church, the community of believers called and ordained to action and service in the world. I am part of this community.

I believe in the Spirit, God's wisdom and guidance in my life, calling me into ministry with the community around me. I open myself to the Spirit's leading.

I believe in the Christ, God present in the world, teaching, healing, and leading me into eternal life. I am a disciple of Jesus' way.

I believe in God, Three in One, whose plan and purpose is the ground of my being. I dedicate my life to God. This is the most important relationship in my life! Amen.

HYMN OF DEDICATION: "In Christ There Is No East or West"

BENEDICTION

Friends, go from this place with a new understanding of your world and of your neighbor. Walk in the way of the Christ, whom we share, and the blessings of Shalom go with you. Amen.

CONGREGATIONAL RESPONSE: "Shalom Chaverim"

POSTLUDE

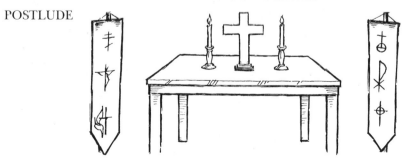

TRINITY SUNDAY

The Feast of the Trinity has been observed in various locales of the church since the tenth century. The celebration was extended to the whole Latin church in the fourteenth century. The Eastern church honors the Trinity during Pentecost, but in the Western church, the first Sunday after Pentecost is set aside to honor the Trinity.

As a faith statement, the Trinity was formalized at the Council of Constantinople in 382 C.E.: God is Three in One. Thus, the focus of this feast day is on the Trinity, the unity of Three persons in One Godhead. This is a day of celebration and praise, giving glory to our Triune God.

GATHER

- white material
- bowl
- oil
- liquid embroidery paint or felt
- floating wicks or candles
- altar
- water

WORSHIP NOTES

Prepare the sanctuary according to Sketch A. Remove the usual cross and candles from the altar. Create an altar cloth from the white material (burlap, sheet, or linen). Cut the material so that a large piece covers the top of the altar, and three segments fall over the front (see diagram). Using cut-out felt or liquid paint, afix the symbols of each attribute of God to a section of the cloth. This symbolizes three in one.

In the middle of the altar, place a bowl containing water and oil. It is possible to purchase a floating candle kit, with instructions, in most variety stores. If these are not available, fill the bowl with water and float votive candles on the surface. Light the wicks or candles during the prelude as a symbol of the light of the Living God.

This is a traditional service, for it is a day devoted to a strong Christian faith tradition. The Trinity is one of the bulwarks of our faith, but one that is hard for many people to understand. Keep the service simple and concentrate on praise to God, in all the ways God meets us.

ORDER OF WORSHIP

GATHERING

PRELUDE

CALL TO WORSHIP

L: In the name of God, our Creator, I greet you.

P: In the name of Christ, who has redeemed us, we greet you.

L: Our lives are blessed and sustained by the Spirit who dwells within and among us.

P: Praise be to God, our Source, our Salvation, our Nurture.

All: Amen!

HYMN OF PRAISE: "Holy, Holy, Holy"

OLD TESTAMENT: (Deut. 4:32-40; Isa. 6:1-8; Prov. 8:22-31)

PRAYER OF CONFESSION

O God of us all, we come before you on this Trinity Sunday aware of your greatness, but not quite trusting it. You come to us in so many ways: through the beauty of creation, in the majesty of Christmas and Easter, in the mystery of Pentecost, and in so many very real ways during the ordinary days. Forgive our reluctance to believe. We confess that we often close our eyes to your presence, our ears to your calling. We pray for your miraculous touch, yet when your hand of caring appears, we label it coincidence rather than your providence.

Open us, O God, to the wonder of you: three-in-one. Remind us that you meet us in all avenues of life and that no situation or circumstance can separate us from your care. In Christ's name we pray, Amen.

WORDS OF ASSURANCE

Our God is actively involved with us. We cannot breathe without God's awareness. Rest now, in the sure knowledge that nothing can separate us from God's love. Amen.

ANTHEM (*optional*)

EPISTLE LESSON (II Cor. 13:5-14; Rom. 8:12-17; Rom. 5:1-5)

PRAYERS OF THE PEOPLE with the Lord's Prayer

OFFERING with Doxology

HYMN OF PREPARATION: "Our God Is Like an Eagle"

GOSPEL: Matthew 28:16-20; John 3:1-17; John 16:12-15

SERMON

A simple explanation of the Trinity is often helpful, since this age-old doctrine still confuses many Christians. We do not worship three Gods, as early critics of the movement charged, but one God in varying forms. This is a God striving to be near us, to meet us in every conceivable way. The Divine Creator takes human form to exhibit that God knows all our struggles. This is the human God, going through death and resurrection. This is the holy God, who takes spirit form to be the omnipresent comforter and friend. This is a God of no limitations, God everywhere and always. This is Divine Love in action.

AFFIRMATION OF FAITH

We believe in God, Creator of the universe, Source of all life. Our God is patient. From Creation to the calling of the Israelites, from the messages of Amos and Anna to the proclamations of modern prophets, God is with us, drawing us closer.

We believe in Jesus, the Christ. Born of Mary, he came to live among us: God in human form. His life taught us true possibility, his death taught us conviction, his resurrection taught us power, even over death.

We believe in the Holy Spirit. This is the Comforter whom Jesus promised to send. In the Spirit, we receive guidance and hope. The Spirit lives within and around us. We are never alone.

HYMN OF DEDICATION: "Now on Land and Sea Descending"

BENEDICTION

L: Go forth with the blessing of our Creator—the One who gave you life.

P: We go into the world, sent by our Redeemer—the One who taught us love and compassion.

L: Go with the guidance of the Spirit—the One who sustains you with wisdom and strength.

P: All our days will be blessed with the Life, and the Love, and the Wisdom of God: Creator, Redeemer, Sustainer—one God, touching us in many ways.

All: Praise be to God. Amen.

POSTLUDE

CHRIST THE KING

A s the Christian calendar has developed, the last Sunday of Pentecost marks the end of the year. At that point, the entire story begins to unfold again. The modern church developed the idea of Christ the King Sunday in order to put some resolution on the year, a time to concentrate once again on the Risen Christ before entering Advent's expectation of the newborn Babe.

This service concentrates on Christ the King, the triumphant Jesus who conquered illness, fear, ignorance, and death. It cannot be forgotten, however, that Christ is a humble king, not at all similar to the monarchs of our time. Jesus is our brother, who has walked beside us and experienced all our pain and uncertainty. This Christ is even more worthy of praise because he has conquered all the things that plague us and has risen victorious over them.

GATHER

● altar   ● candles   ● cross   ● crown of thorns
● traditional crown

WORSHIP NOTES

Set up according to Sketch A. Place the cross and candles on the altar as usual. Make a crown of a thorny root or grapevine twigs. Construct a more traditional crown out of cardboard and gold foil, or buy one at a costume store. Place these crowns on opposite corners of the altar, so that they underscore the tension between worldly kingship and divine rule.

After the benediction, lead the congregation in the chorus of "Lift High the Cross."

ORDER OF WORSHIP

GATHERING
PRELUDE

CALL TO WORSHIP

L: Joyfully, let us come before God with thanksgiving.

P: Our God rules over the whole earth, from the ocean floors to the cloud-draped mountain peaks.

L: All of Creation was made by God, who still is in control.

P: Come, let us kneel before God, our Provider, joining the world in worship.

HYMN OF PRAISE: "O For a Thousand Tongues to Sing"

OLD TESTAMENT: (Jer. 23:1-6; Ezek. 34:11-16, 20-24; II Sam. 5:1-5)

PRAYER OF CONFESSION

O Divine Ruler, forgive us when we misunderstand your ways. Expecting you to come with might, we find instead that you come with love. We live in a world where the privileged rule and money is king, but you show us the power of compassion and the strength of servant-hood. Help us to live in the reflection of your ways. Teach us to serve, rather than to expect service, that the world may truly understand your kingdom. Amen.

WORDS OF ASSURANCE

The One who rules with justice and strength also offers forgiveness to all. As forgiven people, we go forth to serve.

EPISTLE: (Rev. 1:46-48; I Cor. 15:20-28; Col. 1:11-20)

PRAYERS OF THE PEOPLE with the Lord's Prayer

OFFERING with Doxology

HYMN OF PREPARATION: "There's Something About That Name"

GOSPEL: (John 18:33-37; Matt. 25:31-46; John 12:9-19)

SERMON

This is an in-between time. Advent has not yet begun, though the merchants act as if Christmas were here. We are on the threshold of the new Christian year. Remind people that Christly kingship is not to be compared to the monarchies of this world. Christ's humble beginning, life, and death are a paradigm for us. Why are we proud? We follow a humble servant-king. Spend time contrasting the powers and leaders of this world with the humble Jesus.

AFFIRMATION OF FAITH

We believe in God, our Creator and Protector. We believe in the Jesus of the Gospels, whose life was given to others, whose kingdom consisted of uneducated, hard-working people. Jesus taught his band of followers to care for those labeled "unattractive" by society. We struggle to be faithful, remembering Jesus' promise that the first shall be last and the last shall be first.

We reaffirm our commitment to this type of king, whose kingdom gains new life each time we love the unlovable and serve the downtrodden.

We believe in the Holy Spirit, sent by Christ to encourage us as we draw closer to the kingdom. Amen.

HYMN OF DEDICATION: "Jesus Shall Reign"

BENEDICTION

L: The King of Glory has shown us his great power.

P: The Prince of Peace has led us on the Way.

L: The Lord of Love has blessed us with his touch.

P: The Humble One has taught us servanthood.

ALL: Praise be to Christ: Emmanuel, with us now.

BENEDICTION RESPONSE: "Lift High the Cross" (chorus)

POSTLUDE

APPENDIX

HISTORICAL PERSPECTIVE

I t is hard to remember, in this day of crystal cathedrals and tabernacle choirs, that our faith sprang from a small beginning. A tiny nucleus was commissioned at the beginning of our history, and all that we have become is a result of the efforts of that tiny group.

If any formal liturgies existed in that early movement, none of them survived intact. Traces of hymns and sermons, such as the Magnificat in Luke, were probably quoted from other sources when the text was set down in written form.

In the ante-Nicene period (to 325 C.E.), worshipers met in private homes. The Lord's Supper first was elevated above the common meal, then later became a completely separate service. The general public was welcome at the *synaxis,* or meeting, which consisted of Scripture readings interspersed with hymns from the psalms, followed by a time of prayer, a sermon relating the text to everyday life, another prayer, and ended with a benediction by the bishop. At that time the unbaptized worshipers were dismissed so that the Eucharist, or "thanks giving," could begin. Only confirmed Christians could participate in the greeting, kiss of peace, Great Prayer, and Lord's Supper.

With the post-Nicene period (325–604 C.E.), the Christian era began. Services were moved to a separate building for worship, and so many of the general public had become baptized Christians that division of the worship service ceased.

The order of worship continued to expand until it reached three hours in length! Thus during the early Middle Ages, church officials cut the ritual of the service. Unfortunately, this paved the way for strict clericalism: lay participation declined, congregational singing and the importance of the sermon dwindled, and accent was placed on the miracle of the Eucharist rather than on Christ's life in and with the community. A general attitude of human unworthiness prompted the development of the rood screen, a symbol of division between the people and God, or the priest. Fewer people understood the Latin words of the mass. Once a year at Easter, believers were mandated to commune. As in the ante-Nicene time, a separate service developed: the Prone. Celebrated in the vernacular, it involved a service of prayer and praise with preaching. Days and feasts for minor saints multiplied, obscuring the central Sunday worship and the celebration of the major feasts.

The sixteenth century brought the Reform movement. Congregational participation increased, but worship kept its individualistic, subjective attitude. Martin Luther emphasized Sunday worship, along with the major feasts of Christ, over and above the other festivals. Luther and John Calvin tried to reunify sermon and sacrament, while Zwingli and the Anabaptists proclaimed the corruption of the whole concept. The Reformers did restore some flexibility to worship.

Several important things arose out of the post-Reformation movement: again, lay participation declined and worship grew rigid; the Christian calendar met with mixed use. On the positive side, pews were added, and Cranmer developed *The Book of Common Prayer,* giving English worshipers more chance for participation. The Wesleys emphasized preaching, Eucharist, and hymnody.

The true return to the original liturgical form came in the 1800s. While the Benedictines studied the reforms of the Council of Trent (1545–1563 C.E.), they recovered the Patristic forms from the first six centuries and began to relearn those old forms. This new insight brought a heightened interest in liturgy and worship. Not until the twentieth century did the emphasis on corporate worship surface again. The ecumenical three-year lectionary added to the unity. Word, sacrament, order, and mission came together once more, resulting in a unification of Christ's historical and theological significance. Again, baptism rose to prominence, and flexibility returned to worship.

And so our Christian calendar spreads before us as it has been developed over two millennia. From tiny, secretive group meetings in believers' homes, through eras of grand cathedrals and ritualized language, we have come full circle to ecumenical dialogue and liturgy based on research into our core beginnings. We began with a simple pattern: primary worship on Sunday, service of prayer and fasting on Wednesday and Friday, holy feast days on Easter and Pentecost. Ascension Day, the Feast of the Nativity, and other now common days came about later.

Now we have a full calendar, including the holy days of Christ and the special days of our worldwide church. The divine-human dialogue carries on through our time as we attempt to be true to our history and plan for our ecumenical future: no longer one tiny secretive band, but still one Body of the Risen Christ.

THE PEACEABLE KINGDOM

A CHRISTMAS MEDITATION

Several years ago, in a small town in Vermont called Valispree, the council decided to build a zoo. Oh, they already had the sort of zoo most little cities have—an elephant, a few bears and lions, a giraffe, a regional snake collection, birds, an assortment of farm animals, and a deer or two. But when the mayor went to San Diego on business, he was enthralled by their natural-habitat zoological park.

"Valispree must have one!" he proclaimed. "It would be so much better for our animals *and* be beautiful for our citizens, too."

So the city council set about hiring a park ranger and a construction crew. Landscapers researched the natural habitat of each species and carpenters erected shelters for each one. To make it even more authentic, electricians borrowed the idea of low-voltage fences from local farmers; this would condition the animals to remain within their territory without enclosing them behind chain-link fences.

Animal specialists researched nutrition and developed a well-balanced feeding program for each species. Thus, they could reduce staff time and danger by placing the proper amounts and combinations of food on conveyor belts which ran through each animal's area.

The project took exactly one year to complete. The zoological park ranger was so proud! She had overseen a small project that could serve as a model for cities everywhere. And the townspeople thought it was Christmas arriving early!

One sunny day in mid-August, the park ranger opened the gates to the largest crowd the zoo had ever hosted. People who hadn't lived in Valispree for years came back to see this new sight. And no one in town missed it.

As afternoon passed to early evening, however, the electricity began to lag. There was one power surge, then the current stopped almost completely. The park ranger sent her maintenance crew to investigate and calmed herself. This was no time to panic! Lives could be in danger! She was not sure how many minutes would pass before the last few volts of electricity would flow through the fence wires. The plan was so new that the animals were not fully conditioned yet. It wouldn't take them long to discover the possibility of freedom.

She sent all the park staff people to different posts. The trick would be to get all the visitors out of the park as rapidly as possible without creating a mass panic. *That* would be deadly for everyone, including the animals.

Fortunately, the staff was well trained for such an emergency. Although they also were in a hurry to leave the park, they moved the crowd efficiently toward the gates. Parents held their children's hands, couples held on to each other, everyone made room for the people with handicapping conditions.

In about ten minutes' time, everyone had been escorted out of the park. The staff people rushed to the office to plan a strategy for self-protection and protection of the animals.

As the moments passed, the animals sensed something different in the air. Animals are much more observant than humans. The electrical failure caused the conveyor belts to stop, so the animals spent the first half-hour munching on the food before them. They ate until they were much fuller than usual. The conveyor had never given them such a grand feast!

After awhile, they began to explore. Some of the more timid animals, like the elephants, wandered only a short distance from their shelters. Others, like the lions, who loved a good adventure, wandered about the complex with a lazy sort of gait. They watched for humans, so as not to be taken by surprise, but they enjoyed this newfound freedom. Although timid, sheep also are roaming animals, so when the first sheep wandered out of their space, others soon followed. They ambled around the zoo a little, but didn't go too far; sheep must watch not only for humans, but also for natural enemies. Finally, the lead sheep tired and turned the flock toward home—all but one. Completely unaware of danger, a fasci-nated little lamb stopped to look around and lost sight of the group.

Meanwhile, at the front gate, two adults were beating on the fence, try-ing to gain attention. Their little daughter had let go of her father's hand while they were ushered out of the park. She had been left behind. No words can express her parents' frenzy.

Finally, one of the staff members heard the cries and ran over to find the cause of the distress. She hurried the parents into the office, watch-ing for any danger on the way.

When the ranger heard their story, she and her staff quickly drew up rescue plans. Although each of them recognized the personal danger involved, the plight of the little girl was more important.

In the middle of the park was a commons area, an oasis in the zoo. The little girl was tired. At first, she had been overjoyed with her freedom. The animals fascinated her. And after all the people left, the animals were everywhere! She played with the geese and the snakes, then went looking for more fun. She tried to stay clear of the elephants and giraffe because they were so big. But now the chill of the summer evening was coming and dusk was settling all around her. She missed her parents a little. On her way through the middle of the park to find them, she met the little lost lamb crying for its mother. She patted its fluffy wool and felt its warmth. The only lambs she had ever touched were stuffed toys at the store.

The two small beings drew comfort from each other's presence. Being together reduced their fear, so together, they scampered to the commons and sat on the grass. Soon they grew drowsy, but just as the little girl's eyes began to droop, she felt something nuzzle her back. She turned around to find the cutest lion cub she had ever seen. It looked just like a large brown kitten, but its eyes were so big and brown. When the cub yawned, she marveled that such a tiny animal could have so many sharp teeth. Because she was playing with both of them, the little cub and the little lamb seemed content to play together. As they played, a large mother lion ambled slowly toward them. She had been keeping a close watch on her cub. She sniffed at the little girl, but because her stomach was full, she paid little attention to the lamb.

Having had such a feast when the conveyor belt stopped, all the animals were drowsy. First the little lamb went to sleep, then the cub. The little girl lay her head on the lamb's fleece, put her arm around the lion cub, and soon she too was fast asleep. The mother lion walked around them once and then lay down, encircling them with her warmth. The four slept on as the August sun disappeared from the sky.

It seemed to the child's parents that an eon had passed since the staff had gone in search of their little girl. They tried to rid their minds of the most horrible possibilities. They tried to offer each other hope.

The ranger and two of her people rounded the bend on their third trek around the park. Never before had they realized just how much ground this small park covered. As they approached the commons en route back to the office, they glimpsed a group of animals lying on the grass. Quietly, they drew closer. There lay the little girl, surrounded by a lamb, a lioness, and her cub. By now, most of the animals had returned to their own areas for rest and a little more food. One of the staff members remembered that their search had revealed a missing lamb. They had not yet taken inventory of the lions.

Reluctantly, the staff members returned to the office to inform the parents that the child had been found. The ranger insisted on staying near the commons alone. They all knew the danger was far from over, that wild animals have an innate sense of danger and can sense a human's fear from a long distance. The ranger chose a hiding place and watched the group. She tried to remember all her training in animal behavior. She tried to muster all her courage.

At a sound, she looked up to see the child's mother running down the path. She had guessed that the mother had waited as long as she could. Now was the time. At the footfalls, the mother lion looked up. Her eyes met those of the child's mother, and the woman stopped. She too knew that it would be fatal to snatch her child from the group. The lion might maul all of them. The two adults stood dumbfounded.

At that moment, the ZZZT of electrical current traveled around the fence and the lights burned into the night. Coupled with her hunger, it was just enough disturbance to cause the little girl to awaken. She hugged the little lion cub at her side, then reached behind her to pat the little lamb beneath her head. She stretched and looked around. Her eyes followed the gaze of the lioness until they met those of her mother. Overjoyed, she sprang up and ran to her, wanting to introduce her mother to these new friends. She grabbed her mother's hand to drag her back to the scene. All eyes were on the human mother and daughter. As she lifted her daughter in her arms, the mother had some unearthly sense that the mother lion understood this love and protection, even across the lines of the species. She did not go any closer to the animals, but, with a slow nod from the ranger, she did allow her daughter to say good-bye to her friends. The little human thanked the lamb for providing a pillow on which she could rest. She thanked the cub for being her security blanket. She thanked the mother lion for her warmth.

The ranger watched from the distance as the human animals walked away hand in hand. She watched as the mother lion licked the cub and prodded it back to their den. Finally, she went to pick up the lamb and carried it back to its flock. As she placed the small animal beside its mother, she shook her head and said to the earth, the stars, and to anyone who cared to hear, "And the little child shall lead them."

MILK AND HONEY RECIPE

FOR USE WITH BAPTISM OF OUR LORD SERVICE

- 1 Tablespoon honey
- 1 Tablespoon milk
- 6 Tablespoons flour

Stir milk and honey until well blended. Add enough flour to create a pie-crust consistency. Turn mixture onto one half of a sheet of aluminum foil. Fold the other half of the foil over the dough and roll or pat the dough until thin and flat. Uncover the crust and place it and the foil on a cookie sheet or pie pan. Bake for 8-10 minutes in a conventional oven set at 350°. (Microwaves tend to make the dough dry and can burn the honey.)

Remove dough and let it stand until cool. Lift from the foil and break into 30 or 40 small pieces. Store in an air-tight container until time for use.

Serve on a paten or plate at the appointed time during the service.

VARIATIONS

—If more uniform pieces are desired, use a pizza cutter to serrate the dough before baking.

—Add 1 to 1½ tablespoons of shortening if a flakier crust is desired.

—To make a paste instead of bread, use only 2 tablespoons flour in the mixture. This may be served on small crackers or placed in a dignified bowl or chalice-like vessel. The celebrant may use small wooden or plastic spoons, serving each of the baptized in a method resembling intinction.

ON THE MOUNTAIN

A GUIDED MEDITATION FOR TRANSFIGURATION SUNDAY

Breathe slowly and allow your breath to fill your body. Then let it go. Breathe in and let go. Spend a few moments looking over the hiking gear before you. Think about the trek up Mount Hermon. When Jesus invites you to go with him, what will you need? The mountain is snow-covered, and the scenery is beautiful. Breathe deeply and let go. Slowly close your eyes and enter the world of your imagination. In your mind, draw a picture of the scene. Followers have been crowding around for days. Everyone is exhausted. Jesus is the first to say he needs to get away. Breathe deeply of this new air. Feel your tiredness. Feel the muscles in your body—your feet, your legs, your shoulders, your neck. Relax in your chair. Let it hold you. Relax and breathe deeply, fully, slowly. Then let it go.

Jesus has invited you and two friends to climb up out of the city. Are you rested? Do you have your gear? How heavy is it? Make sure it is well packed and easy to carry. Time to go. Put on your knapsack and join the group.

Breathe deeply of the fresh air. Caesarea Philippi is a beautiful city, but there have been so many people! Hear the crunch of the earth beneath your feet. No wonder David described God as a shepherd. You can feel God close to you here. It's a good thing you wore hiking boots with good tread and thick soles. The rocky patches of ground are sharp.

It's a quiet trip. Climbing makes everyone breathe a little harder and the silence is so nice. You have been surrounded by people talking, people needing so much, ever since you started traveling with Jesus. It feels good to get away. Feel the cool, fresh air. Check your knapsack. How does it feel on your shoulders and back? Relax your shoulders and let them fall. Jesus is a good, strong walker. It takes some effort to keep up with him. He hardly ever carries anything. It makes his travel easier, and he laughs and says he doesn't need anything. Did you bring too much? You can stop and drop something off. We will be coming back this way.

Jesus didn't say, but it's obvious he is going up to pray. That is what he always does when he goes off from the crowd. It seems to nourish him.

We're midway up the mountain now. The snow is sparse—little patches here and there. It is odd to see it. Stop to pick up a handful, just to feel the chill on your skin. Such a marvelous thing nature is!

Here we are at the top. Stop to get your breath. Maybe look for a rock to drop your sack and sit down. It is refreshing to be up so high. You can see for miles. Such a beautiful country. You can feel yourself slowing down. Drowsiness is overtaking you. Your eyes are heavy. You may stretch a bit. Relax. Let your body go. Relax. Relax. Breathe deeply. Let it go.

Something rouses you. You must have slept. A light is coming from somewhere. A bright light shining on your face. Where? You sit up and look around. At first your eyes won't focus. At first, all you can see is light. Slowly you recognize the face of Jesus, his body, his clothing glistening with such a bright light. It is almost overwhelming. But two men are with him—your two friends? No, this is no one you recognize. Look. Look. Something jars your memory. Something familiar. Elijah! Elijah! The great prophet Elijah is talking with Jesus. Oh, you must rub your eyes! And the other one—Moses! The great liberator, Moses. Moses of the law! Jesus, Elijah, and Moses are shimmering, standing a little apart, talking. Ah, if it's a dream, don't pinch yourself. At least it is a good dream!

One of your friends rushes over to them. You must choose whether to join them or just watch.

"We should build three tabernacles," your friend whispers. "One for each of them. We could live on this mountaintop forever!" Your whole body tingles with awe and excitement. Jesus, Elijah, and Moses together, engulfed in light!

Now you look up to see a great cloud slowly gliding toward the spot. You watch as it stops.

"This is my Son. Hear him."

Could that have been the voice of one of your friends? It didn't sound like their voices, nor like the voice of Jesus. It was a rich, deep voice, the kind you can feel in your own chest when you put your ear to the ground. Your head is whirling, but you stopped conscious thought some time ago.

As you watch, the cloud moves away and the light begins to fade.

Jesus is alone, still glowing, still looking refreshed, but the luster is gone. He motions to gather your things and follow him.

You are torn. It is hard to leave a place of such glories. But Jesus is right. There is still much to do. Always more work, more people to see. So much need.

You gather your things and laugh at all the items you could have left behind. Next time, you'll take Jesus' advice. You will bring only a walking stick.

Walking downhill is always easier than climbing, but you are floating on the experience just past. Jesus lets you know that this is a secret among the four of you. It will be hard not to tell your friends, your spouse.

As you draw closer and closer to level ground, you begin to think about what Jesus told you before any of this happened. The memory of it brings a heaviness to your step. It didn't make any sense then, and it surely doesn't now. Why would anyone want to harm such a magnificent man? The world must be crazy! Suddenly you stop. It is almost impossible to put one foot before the other. Why not just go and live at the top of the mountain? Why go back at all? Even in good times, the level ground cannot compare to this. Maybe we could just avoid the pain and turmoil. Maybe Jesus wouldn't need to die. You can feel his eyes on you. Slowly you begin to walk again. You have lived and traveled together long enough now to know what Jesus is thinking, you can feel him pulling on you. The time of prayer and exaltation has been wonderful. Now it is time to turn that exaltation into service.

You fall into step with the others. Soon you will be down the hill. The things you dropped off on the way up don't seem important any more. You leave them.

Gradually, ever so slowly, you reach the bottom of the mountain. It has been a long and eventful trip. As the other disciples gather around, you drop your knapsack and sit down. Breathe deeply. Let it go. And gradually, as you are ready, open your eyes and come back to this room.

LETTER TO A SISTER

AN EASTER STORY

Dear Sister,
I have been in such a state lately, I could not stop to write. Please forgive me. When you hear all that has happened, you will understand.

Two days after the government killed Jesus, I arose at the crack of dawn. I hadn't slept for days. But they just couldn't keep me away from that tomb, no matter how many legions they had guarding the door! It was so hard to leave him there, to leave his body after they took him down from that torturous cross. It's the scene I see when I close my eyes and try to sleep—that hideous scene: his sweat and his agony, the drops of blood caking on his body in the hot sun, the ugly crowd jeering, the Roman soldiers, stoic and rough. But we stayed; his mother even stayed through the whole thing, standing there at the foot of that Roman cross. I couldn't stay, but I couldn't leave. They said it was a blessing that he had died so quickly. Most just hang there for days. They had tortured him so that he had lost a massive amount of blood. Oh, sister, I hope I live to forget that scene. It just keeps playing over and over in my head. I was so ashamed that I couldn't do anything to help him. I couldn't save him. It hurts so much.

I'm afraid I wasn't very worshipful the next day. I just kept remembering that they had condemned him in a Temple. Will my resentment ever go away? I was so confused and angry. But he wouldn't want that. He forgave them all, even in the middle of all his pain. Why can't I? Oh, Jesus! It was the longest sabbath I have ever known. Every minute seemed to last for hours. But eventually it passed, and we were free to go. James' mother, Mary, and—was it Salome or Joanna? Oh, I just can't remember—had helped me prepare the spices before the sabbath. We met, then, the day after the sabbath when the sun was just coming up. It was obvious that they hadn't slept, either. Together, we took the spices and set off for the cemetery.

And we were all a little scared. We asked a stream of the "what if" questions: "What if the guards won't let us in?"; "What if we can't get the stone away from the opening?" It probably increased our worry, but facing our fears was better than feeling the terrible emptiness of grief. We walked rapidly, but it seemed to take forever.

As we drew closer, two Roman guards came running toward us. We used all our fortitude to steel ourselves against their attack, but they just ran past us, their faces ashen and haunted. We kept walking, our curiosity spurring us forward. Then I saw the stone lying on the ground beside the entrance to the tomb! My heart sank!

"What have they done to my Jesus now?"

Anger and fear and confusion overtook me. I just kept chanting, "What shall we do? What shall we do?"

One of the others suggested that I run to get Peter and John. They were closest to Jesus. Maybe they would know what to do.

Suddenly my feet were running without control. I got to the men in a moment and tried to pant out the awful truth, but I couldn't stop. I grabbed their sleeves and pulled them with all my might. When they finally understood that something was wrong at the tomb, they outran me and pushed their way into the tomb. It was absolutely empty. Only the burial shroud and some cloths were folded neatly at the top and the bottom of the slab where Jesus' body had been. Nothing else. We were dazed. No one could speak. The two men staggered out of the tomb and wandered away. In despair and confusion, I just stood still and sobbed. This was too much. Hadn't we been through enough? Now they have stolen Jesus' body!

In my dazed hysteria, I peered into the tomb for the first time. Through my tears, I saw two figures suddenly appear. Their robes were dazzlingly white. One sat at the head of the slab, the other at the foot. I blinked and wiped my eyes. Mary had to hold me up.

"Don't be afraid," they said. "Why are you crying?"

Were these two men stupid? How could anyone not know?

"They have taken away my Lord," I shouted. "I don't know what they have done with him!"

I felt my head spin. I turned and almost bumped into someone standing behind me.

"Who are you looking for?" he asked.

Was this another plot against Jesus? Were these men and this gardener part of it? They were surely playing with my emotions. I demanded to know where they had taken Jesus.

"I will go and get him," I vowed.

"Mary!" he spoke my name.

Instantly I knew that voice. Joy flowed through me! Peace overwhelmed me. *This was* Jesus!

"Teacher!" I couldn't believe my eyes. My head was swimming. I started to grab his robe, but he stepped back ever so slightly.

"Mary, I must ascend to my God before you touch me. Go tell the others you have seen me, that I have been raised to Life, just as I told you. I will go ahead of you now and meet all of you in Galilee. Peace be with you, Mary."

Then he was gone. I looked at Mary and the others. Their eyes carried the same wonder I felt. What had just happened? Was it true? Had we been asleep and dreaming? Were we drunk with grief? I got up and looked in the tomb again. Sister, I tell you, everything was as it had been—the slab and the folded sheets! I could still feel his presence, and I could still hear him speak my name. All three of us ran to tell the others.

Well, sister, it was the joy of hearing him speak my name that got me through the next couple of days. You would think they would have believed us. Maybe not one woman with such a fantastic story—but *three* witnesses! Sometimes it just doesn't pay to be a woman, I guess. I ran ahead and told them. No one believed me, not even Peter and John. Gradually, though, they all came around. Some, like Thomas, are still holding out, but Jesus will get to him also.

I'm kind of ashamed, you know. After all, he told us time and time again what would happen. Why would we even doubt? Why would we be so surprised when it did happen, exactly as he told us? You'd think that we, the ones who were closest to him, would have understood. He told us so many times about resurrection, about defeating death, about returning to life with God. I guess it was just too new. We just didn't get it until the evidence was right there, standing in front of us.

O sister, I wish you could have been there! When I think about seeing him, hearing him say my name, I can feel the relief and the joy fill me from head to toe.

I apologize for writing such a self-involved letter. I just had to tell you everything! I do think of you often. I miss talking with you and hope to be back in Magdela with you soon. In the meantime, I remain your loving sister,

Mary

PETER'S MESSAGE

A PARAPHRASE FOR PENTECOST

Brothers and sisters, please give me your attention. You who live here in Jerusalem, and you who have come because of your religious celebration of Shabuoth, I am Peter, and these are the other apostles. We walked with Jesus, and he taught us many things. Let us try to explain what is happening here. No one is drunk. You don't need to worry about that. It is nine o'clock in the morning! Who would be intoxicated at this hour? No, this is that event about which our prophet Joel told us. You remember? He said that God had told him:

> In the final phase of creation I will pour out my Spirit on everyone. Your daughters and your sons will give voice to my words; your old wise ones will dream dreams. Even my servants—both women and men—will receive my Spirit and tell my message. I will perform miracles in the skys and work wonders on the earth. You will see blood and fire and thick smoke, and the sun will be blood red before I rest with the world. During that time, I will hear those who call out to me, and I will save them. (Joel 2:28-32)

Do you remember those words, sisters and brothers of Israel? What could this miraculous thing be, but that event which Joel told us about. You saw all the wondrous things Jesus did. God did those things through Jesus. Yes, our Jesus of Nazareth acted with divine authority. You should know this! It happened right before your eyes!

It was also part of God's plan that Jesus would suffer because of your ignorance and jealousy. It was part of the original plan that he would be slain by those who have no relationship with God. But the divine plan went much further. Death could not hold Jesus. God released him from death's power. King David—our own ancestor—said:

> In front of me, I always saw God; I will not worry because God is near me. That knowledge fills me with joy. Even with all my human limitations and frailties, I am filled with hope. I know that God will not abandon me in

death nor allow me to rot in the grave. God has shown me the way that leads to Life, and God's presence fills me with joy. (Ps. 16:8-11)

Sisters and brothers, let me tell you about our own great King David. He died and was buried right here with us. King David was a prophet. He knew and believed God's promises to him—David was the fulfillment of one of God's promises to Israel, and he believed God's promise to make one of his descendants a king. Because David believed God's promises, he knew what the future would bring. And so, he talked of the resurrection of the Messiah. He said, and I repeat, "God did not abandon him to the world of death and darkness, nor allow him to rot in the grave" (Ps. 16:10).

Now, we are all witnesses to this fact: God raised Jesus from death. Jesus has been raised from death to return to God. And now he has sent the Holy Spirit, just as he promised. *That* is what you see happening around you. The Holy Spirit's gifts have been poured out upon us. David did not go up to heaven, as Jesus did. David said, "God said to my Savior, sit here at my right side until I put your enemies in their places" (Ps. 110:1).

People of Israel, you must acknowledge that this Jesus of Nazareth, this man whom you crucified, is the Messiah, the One we have awaited for so long.

I know this is confusing. But if each of you turns your back on the sin and ignorance of your past life, you can start again. When you present yourself to be baptized in Jesus' name, the sins of your past will be fully forgiven, and the Holy Spirit will become part of you. God has made this promise to you, to your children, and to the whole earth. God's blessings are here for all who hear the call.

Brothers and sisters, this is your chance to save your lives! Punishment awaits those who continue in their selfish ways—a punishment which results in death and darkness. You must believe me! Come, be baptized! Come and receive God's gift.

Postscript—Acts 2:41 NRSV: "So those who welcomed his message were baptized, and that day about three thousand persons were added."

ALTERNATIVE HYMN SUGGESTIONS

Epiphany

All Who Love and Serve Your City
Give Me a Clean Heart, That I May Serve Thee

Baptism of Our Lord

I Shall Not Be Moved
God of Grace and God of Glory
Be Thou My Vision
Master, Speak, Thy Servant Heareth

Transfiguration

Christ, upon the Mountain Peak
Christ, Whose Glory Fills the Sky
O Wondrous Sight, O Vision Fair
Fairest Lord Jesus
Where He Leads Me

Shrove Tuesday

Joy Is Like the Rain
Peace Like a River

Ash Wednesday

Jesus Walked This Lonesome Valley
I Surrender All
There Is a Balm in Gilead

Palm Sunday

All Glory, Laud, and Honor
Once to Ev'ry One and Nation

Maundy (Holy) Thursday

Fill My Cup, Lord
Let Us Break Bread Together

Good Friday

Sometimes I Wish My Eyes Had Never Been Opened
At the Cross
It Is Well with My Soul

Easter Vigil

He Is Lord
Lord of the Dance
My Lord, What a Morning
Morning Has Broken
Amen

Ascension Day

God Is Working His Purpose Out
Great Is Thy Faithfulness
(those listed under Easter Vigil)

Pentecost

I'm Gonna Sing When the Spirit Says Sing
I Am the Church
Pass It On
Walls That Divide Are Broken Down

Christian Unity

Blest Be the Tie That Binds
We Shall Overcome
The Church's One Foundation
Turn Your Eyes upon Jesus
This Is My Song
(those listed under Pentecost)

Trinity Sunday

Father, I Adore You
God Is Working His Purpose Out
God of Earth and Sea and Heaven

Christ the King

O How I Love Jesus
Lift High the Cross
He Is Lord
All Who Love and Serve Your City

HYMN RESOURCES

Everflowing Streams: Songs for Worship, ed. Ruth C. Duck and Michael G. Bausch. New York: Pilgrim Press, 1981.

The Hymnal of the United Church of Christ. Philadelphia: United Church Press, 1974.

Songs of Zion. Nashville: Abingdon Press, 1981.

The United Methodist Hymnal. Nashville: The United Methodist Publishing House, 1989.